Unsearchable Riches

Unsearchable Riches

W. Vernon Higham

CHRISTIAN FOCUS PUBLICATIONS

ISBN 1-85792-768-0

Published in 2003 by
Christian Focus Publications, Geanies House,
Fearn, Ross-shire, IV20 1TW, Scotland

www.christianfocus.com

Cover design by Alister MacInnes

Printed and bound by
Cox & Wyman, Reading, Berkshire

Contents

Foreword 7

1 The Living God 15

2 The King 29

3 The Choice 45

4 The Problem 59

5 The New Creature 73

6 The Risen Lord 89

7 The Narrow Way 99

8 The Warfare 117

9 The Promise 131

10 The Consummation 145

11 The Inheritance 155

FOREWORD

THE RICHES OF GRACE

'That I may know him, and the power of his resurrection, and the fellowship of his sufferings, being made conformable unto his death' (Phil. 3:10).

Scripture has a very disturbing influence, and has affected men and women deeply all along the ages. Men have stood condemned by its pages, and men have come to a saving knowledge and experience of the Lord Jesus Christ when its truths have been applied in the power of the Holy Spirit. It is essential that we are honest with ourselves regarding spiritual matters. In this realm more than in any other we dare not be neglectful, for on our true response to God depends our eternal destiny.

What are our hearts really like? On the rare occasions when all the busyness of life is still, and we have time to stop and consider ourselves, what do we discover? 'As a man thinketh in his heart, so is he' (Prov. 23:7). This is a disturbing and a sobering thought, because we do not like what we find.

When, by the enlightenment of the Holy Spirit, we begin to understand something of the depravity of the human mind and heart, we are horrified, and wonder if there is sufficient grace to deal with such sin. We begin to realise that true religion must deal with the depths of our hearts if we are to have lasting peace with God. We want peace with God. We want the kind of knowledge that enlightens, and an experience that affects our whole being, so that we may know and feel the mercy and saving work of God.

There are times when God draws near to us, and there is a stirring in our innermost being, responding to spiritual things. Yet so readily we forget, so quickly we turn to the attractive playthings of this world. Or maybe, we may quieten our consciences with a milder and less demanding form of Christianity. And then God has to place us yet again in some situation that will demonstrate our frailty and our helplessness, in order to move our hearts to cry out to Him.

There are riches in Christ that have no limit. If we should try to measure them, our measuring rods could not begin to estimate His boundless store. Paul, in writing of his experience in preaching the gospel, expresses the feeling of awe that he felt, 'Unto me, who am less than the least of all saints, is this grace given, that I should preach among the Gentiles the unsearchable riches of Christ' (Eph. 3:8). It seems so wonderful that God should quicken the spiritually dead, grant them forgiveness by the atonement of Jesus Christ, impart His righteousness to them, and give unworthy people everlasting life. Such grace, such mercy, overwhelms the mind of the apostle by its very magnitude. He seeks to describe the love of Christ, and finds that it defies description. Words fail, and 'lost in wonder, love and praise' he implores that God Himself should manifest His glory to the Ephesian Christians.

When God is moving in the soul, our hearts are moved with wonder as we look upon this small corner of His work. 'When I consider thy heavens, the work of thy fingers, the moon and the stars, which thou hast ordained; what is man, that thou art mindful of him? and the son of man, that thou visitest him?' (Ps. 8:3,4). To think that this glorious God of creation is mindful of us! He is as aware of all our needs and the slightest tremor of our innermost being as He is of vast galaxies. The riches of His grace, like the vastness of His creation, are unsearchable; and yet in one small corner of His grace He works in our hearts, bringing healing to our souls.

In the Bible we find many wonderful accounts of the dealings of God with His people. The truths taught in the Bible are consistent. We find a glorious unity of all aspects of the power and character of God and in all His work as these are portrayed for us in His holy and authoritative Word. These glorious doctrines about God are living information about Himself, the author and source of all being. When the Holy Spirit applies these truths to our quickened souls and enlightened understanding, they fill our whole being with truth. Each doctrine warms our hearts and thrills our understanding. It is important that we allow these truths to do their work in us, and that we do not merely assimilate them on an intellectual level. We are past masters at evasion, and we can allow even the truth itself to be a cold system of theology, which touches our hearts very little and affects our lives even less.

The wonderful miracle in all this is that we can become rich. Whatever our station in life, whatever our ability, we can be rich towards God. There is no need for us to be spiritual paupers. Whether we are or not becomes evident in times of stress – do we then apply the truth that we say that we know? I shall always remember my paternal grandfather for one thing. Every time he stayed with us he bought us an expensive utensil for the home, and then he would tell us that it was the best on the market and that it was to be used and not stored away. I can remember him buying a teapot, which lasted very well, even with the heavy use that you can imagine a Welsh teapot would get! He would say, 'Buy a good thing and make good use of it.' The teachings of Holy Scripture are the best that could ever be; they are above price, and they are meant to be put to use in our lives. How many teapots have ended up in a display cabinet, and then when eventually brought into use have failed to stand the heat of boiling water? How many doctrines have we paraded before men, only to find that they fail us in our hour of need because they have not permeated our hearts and lives? We need to know our doctrines, but we must also apply them to our hearts and use them in our lives, as vital evidence that the grace of God is at work in us, and so that we might stand in the day of trouble. 'Ho, every one that thirsteth, come ye to the waters, and he that hath no money; come ye, buy, and eat; yea, come, buy wine and milk without money and without price. Wherefore do ye spend money for that which is not bread? and your labour for that which satisfieth not? hearken diligently unto me, and eat ye that which is good, and let your soul delight itself in fatness' (Isa. 55:1,2).

Deep in my heart there is a sigh,
A longing, Lord, for Thee,
To know the depths that in Thee lie,
The grace of Calvary.
O grant that I might understand
Thy glorious mystery,
More of Thyself, and by Thy hand
Obedience stir in me.

Thy living power I long to prove
In resurrection might,
With overcoming grace to move
Each sin that dims this light.
O grant that I may find the source
Of hidden strength and stay,
Which flows from Thee, and on its course
O draw my soul each day.

There is a fellowship of pain
Deep in Thy heart of love,
Of suffering sweet, eternal gain,
The tears of heaven above.
O grant me, Lord, to feel this joy,
These tremors of Thy grace;
Engraved by Thee, none can destroy
The riches I embrace.

Then lead me in this wondrous way
To die to self and sin;
Now take me, Lord, when Thou dost slay,
and drive Thy grace within.
O grant me now an image sweet
Impressed upon my heart;
With joy I lie beneath Thy feet,
To weep and not depart.

1

THE LIVING GOD

Some years ago my wife and I were on holiday at a seaside resort in Cornwall. One day we ventured out on a sea trip which proved to be most hazardous. A sudden change of weather caused the waves to rise like mountains thus endangering our little boat greatly, so that a lifeboat was sent out to bring us safely back into port. Within a few hours the event was the talking point of many along the quayside, and we found ourselves in conversation with an old sailor and his wife. In discussing the happenings of the day he began to relate a little of his own life and told how he and his wife had lost two sons at sea. Then, looking kindly at his wife he concluded 'We've had our ups and downs, but the Lord, he has been more than good. I really don't know what we would have done without Him'. They had faith in God and He had kept them during their long and tempestuous lives.

Today we see increasingly large numbers of

men and women living as if there were no God, totally unaware of His general providence, neither knowing nor caring that it is He in whom we all 'live, move and have our being'. The result is a society characterised by despair and hopelessness, rebellion against authority and frustration with life. A godless society is aimless and purposeless. The prospect of a life without God is terrifying.

1. The Truth about God

The Existence of God

The Bible does not seek to prove that 'God is,' because that should be obvious to all. Everything that we see and know is the handiwork of the Creator – 'In the beginning God created the heaven and the earth' (Gen. 1:1). Although all men have sufficient ability to conclude that there is a God, they cannot come to a saving knowledge of Him on their own – 'the natural man receiveth not the things of the Spirit of God: for they are foolishness unto him, neither can he know them, because they are spiritually discerned.' (1 Cor. 2:14). It is God who makes Himself known to us, and draws us to Himself by His Holy Spirit. The Spirit reveals these things to us through the Bible, applying its truths to our hearts and minds. This is no ordinary book, but the very word of God to man: 'All Scripture is given by inspiration of God and is profitable for doctrine, for reproof, for correction, for instruction in righteousness: that the man of God may be perfect, throughly furnished unto all good works' (2 Tim. 3:16,17). We believe that the Bible is a book bearing the authority of God, infallible in its teaching and content. Once we leave the pages of Scripture, our concept of God is humanised. We no longer present the God who reveals Himself in its pages as the one true, living God.

The Character of God

In describing the attributes of God we can divide them into His 'natural' and His 'moral' attributes.

The natural attributes

The *natural attributes* are His infinity, His personality, His immutability, His omnipresence, and His omnipotence. By His *infinity* we mean that God knows no limits, as men do, thus in speaking of His love or holiness we can only conclude that the knowledge is too high for us. Paul, in describing the 'length and breadth and depth of the love of God' comes to the point where he can only exclaim 'it passeth knowledge.' This God is completely outside and beyond all concepts of time and space.

It is important to realise that God is a *Person* not a 'thing,' a mere 'being', but that He has a mind, emotions, will, and freedom, though, of course, on a far higher level than our own human understanding of these qualities. He is a God with a very real and definite identity, a fact which we must never lose sight of.

God is *unchanging* and *unchangeable*. When King Hezekiah was on his death bed the prophet Isaiah, the son of Amos, informed him that he would soon die, and advised him to put his house in order. Hezekiah, in deep distress turned his face to the wall, calling on God. God, in His mercy, answered him and told the prophet to 'Go, and say to Hezekiah, Thus saith the Lord, the God of David thy Father, I have heard thy prayer, I have seen thy tears: behold, I will add unto thy days fifteen years' (Isa. 38:5). He reminded Hezekiah that He was still the same God. He was the God of David, 'the God of Abraham, Isaac and Jacob,' the 'same yesterday, today and forever.'

God is *omnipresent* and *omniscient*. We cannot escape from the presence of God. The furthermost parts of His Creation are near to Him. David realises this when He tries to escape from God. Wherever he goes he says of God 'Thou art there'. He realises that God sees into his very heart, that nothing is hidden from Him. Jonah is commanded to go to Nineveh but he is unwilling to go. He endeavours to escape from God by taking a ship to Tarshish from Joppa. Whilst on the voyage a great storm overtakes the ship to the terror of the sailors. They finally single him out as the cause of their trouble and threaten to cast him into the sea. He confesses his guilt and responsibility to the fearful sailors. 'And he said unto them, Take me up and cast me forth into the sea; so shall the sea be calm unto you: for I know that for my sake this great tempest is upon you' (Jonah 1:12). He is cast into the sea but the Lord has prepared a fish to swallow him, and there he prays. 'Then Jonah prayed unto the Lord his God out of the fish's belly' (Jonah 2:1). The Lord then commands him to go to Nineveh. He is delivered from his predicament and goes obediently to that city to declare the Word of the Lord to them. Wherever he goes Jonah cannot escape God, he cannot hide from His all-seeing eye and His wonderful knowledge.

God is *almighty*, and no one can ever be equal with Him. He reigns supreme over all His creation, and all the affairs of nations are in His hand. His power and abilities know no limit. Because of His absolute greatness and supremacy it is both useless and foolish to compare any one with Him. He is omnipotent. To trust in anyone less than God or in anything is to deceive ourselves. Isaiah in demonstrating the futility of idols, and of faith in gods that are not gods, writes of the Almighty, 'To whom will ye liken me, and make me equal, and compare me, that we may be like?... Remember the former things of old: for I am God, and there is none else; I am God, there is none like me... My Counsel shall stand, and I will do all my pleasure' (Isa. 46:5,9,10).

The moral attributes

The moral attributes of God are His goodness, His holiness, and His righteousness. The *goodness* of the Lord is presented to us in the Bible in His merciful and gracious dealings with men. The Psalmist exhorts us: 'to taste and see that the Lord is good' (Ps. 34:8). Peter exhorts young converts to feed on the word of God: 'If so be ye have tasted that the Lord is gracious' (1 Pet. 2:3). During the days of the wandering of the children of Israel in the desert in search of the promised land, the goodness of God is revealed. Water is provided when Moses strikes a rock at the command of God, and their thirst is quenched. Daily manna is provided for their needs as they travel the weary miles. God was good to them. We too, know of this goodness and have proved the wonderful provision of God in our lives. In our distress we have called. He has heard our cry and met our needs. God has been good to us.

The *holiness* of God can be clearly seen throughout the pages of Scripture, and we are made aware of His awful purity. The prophet Isaiah in his experience in the Temple is confronted with the absolute holiness of God. He enters the Temple and sees a vision of God, the train of God's robes filling the building. Seraphims fly around him uttering celestial songs and anthems. This vision has a profound effect upon Isaiah. He becomes conscious of his dreadful unworthiness in the light of God's holiness: 'Then said I, Woe is me! for I am undone; because I am a man of unclean lips, and I dwell in the midst of a people of unclean lips: for mine eyes have seen the King, the Lord of Hosts' (Isa. 6:5).

God's *righteousness* is obvious in all His dealings with Israel as a nation, with individuals within that nation, and with the 'spiritual Israel.' God acts consistently with His righteous and holy laws, and never lowers these standards in all His dealings with men. Because of His righteousness we are made aware of His justice, and of His anger against all unrighteousness and evil.

The Divine Trinity

Our God is a Triune God, Three persons in One, One in Three. To our finite minds this is paradoxical, yet it is a glorious truth which is revealed progressively throughout the Bible. We are first introduced to it in Genesis, 'In the beginning God created the heaven and the earth. And the earth was without form, and void; and darkness was upon the face of the deep. And the Spirit of God moved upon the face of the waters. And God said, Let there be light: and there was light' (Gen. 1:1-3). The Spirit is specifically named here, and the Saviour in John's Gospel 'In the beginning was the Word, and the Word was with God, and the Word was God . . . All things were made by him; and without him was not anything made that was made' (John 1:1,3). When God created man in His own image we read the plural form for God, and again here the sense of a triune God is implied in the account. 'Let us make man in our image, after our likeness' (Gen. 1:26).

There is no doubt about the teaching of Scripture on the divinity of the Father, Son and Holy Spirit. We see the relationship of the work of the Persons of the Triune God in Peter's Epistle when, in describing the work of Salvation, the three persons in the Godhead are named with their respective involvement in this work of grace. He greets those who are 'elect according to the foreknowledge of God the Father, through sanctification of the Spirit, unto obedience and sprinkling of the blood of Jesus Christ' (1 Pet. 1:2). In the Gospel of Matthew when the Lord Jesus Christ spoke to His disciples before He finally ascended to the Father, He gave them their divine commission to preach the gospel. He commanded them to go in the name of the Triune God, and it is in this name and by His power that they went: 'go ye, therefore, and teach all nations, baptising them in the name of the Father, and of the Son, and of the Holy Ghost' (Matt. 28:19). This doctrine is basic to the historic Christian Church.

God the *Father* is often the representative of all three persons in the Trinity, especially in the work of creation and judgment, whereas we ascribe the planning of redemption and providence more particularly to Him. The *Lord Jesus Christ* takes the second place in order in the Trinity. While we are aware that the Father is the source of all things, we know that everything is through the Son. It is Jesus Christ who executes the Father's plan of redemption. All we have and can ever be must be through the mediatorial work of the Son of God. The Son shares with the Father the attributes ascribed to God, but in particular is involved with the work of redemption which necessitated His taking on human flesh, so that He has a nature which is fully divine, and a nature which is fully human; without contradiction they are in glorious harmony in the same person. The *Holy Spirit* shares the same attributes. There are certain works however, that are particularly ascribed to Him. The Holy Spirit applies the work of the Son in us, bringing the things of Christ to us. It is the Holy Spirit who dwells within us, sanctifying us and working out the grace of God in our lives.

2. How this Truth affects us

Encouragement

Because God is omnipresent we are greatly encouraged in our hearts that He will never leave us nor forsake us. It is both a comfort and a challenge to us: a comfort to know that we have a friend who will always be by our side, even in the valley of death itself; a challenge because we are conscious of His presence as a rebuke when we have wandered from the pathway of His will.

Sincerity

God is omniscient, nothing can be hidden from Him: neither our deepest sorrow, nor our secret sin. It is good to know that He can meet the longings of our hearts and help us when others cannot draw near or understand. We also know that our unworthy desires are known to Him and that we cannot pretend before this God. Before Him we must always be honest for nothing is hid from Him.

Strength

His omnipotence is a strength to our lives because we know that the God who is our God is almighty. There is no power that can take us away from Him: to belong to this God is safety indeed. The early Christians again and again proved His wonderful keeping power in the storms and trials of life. 'Who are kept by the power of God, through faith unto salvation ready to be revealed in the last time' (1 Peter 1:5). He is neither fickle nor changeable as we are, but His word is faithful and unchanging like Himself. All His promises are true so that we can gladly and happily rest in the reliability of His word to us.

Challenge

When we consider His goodness, holiness and righteousness, we begin to see that this powerful God has a moral character of purity and beauty. Because this is so, we, too, must learn to desire that which is well pleasing to God. As He increases in our lives so also does our appetite for good things. Our fellowship with Him becomes sweet.

Longing to know Him more

The more we know this wonderful God, the more we want to know Him. We realise that apart from God life is empty and frightening, and that our busy little lives have no meaning as our tiny solar system hurtles through endless space. Amazement replaces perplexity as we begin to appreciate the work of creation in all its vastness, in all its minute detail. Our hearts are drawn out in worship of this Creator God. He gives to life meaning and purpose, coupled with a quiet confidence in the knowledge that He is in control. We know that He does all things well. He is our God and we are His children.

Complete dependence

I can remember as a child being very fond of a song sung by a well-known soloist. We used to play the record continuously at home, yet for years I misapplied the words: 'What is life to me without Thee?' In the song they are addressed to a lover, yet how apt they are when applied to the Lord God. As believers we come to realise that He is 'all in all'; it becomes our chief concern to live to His glory, to be well pleasing to Him. We learn to rejoice in this God, and seek to know Him more and more.

O how I fear Thee, *Living God,*
With deepest, tenderest fears,
And worship Thee with trembling hope
And penitential tears!

How wonderful, how beautiful
The sight of Thee must be,
Thine endless wisdom, boundless power,
And awful purity!

2

THE KING

What a dismal affair life would be if history told no story, if it were just a chain of meaningless events revealing no plan or purpose, guided by nothing but chance. Life itself would be empty and meaningless, and our lives as individuals would be like driftwood floating on the ocean of chaos. The Christian faith, however, points to a God who not only has a distinct character and form, but who is behind the history of men, planning it all and giving it purpose. This God is sovereign.

He is not an indifferent God, who creates at whim and then playfully moves on to something else, leaving man to drift along, mearly led by some vague sense of purpose. Rather, He is a God who both creates and is involved with His creation, so that there is purpose in His actions and sustained interest in their continuance. Always in considering the sovereignty of God we must begin here, with faith in a supreme Being who rules over all that He has made.

1. The Truth about God's Sovereignty

All that exists is His, and nothing can continue to exist except by His permission. The knowledge of this is not attained through our own clever reasoning, but is received from God who has chosen to reveal Himself to us. It is from the Bible that we learn these truths about God. We are given by revelation details concerning His sovereignty which we should never have known of ourselves.

As Christians we believe that there is no one who can ever be compared, or who can ever compete, with this God. However advanced men may be in startling achievement, they and their discoveries still remain part of the creation in which God reigns supreme. He stands alone in triune splendour, the glorious unity of Father, Son and Holy Spirit. Our God is the creator of all that is: the world, the universe and the vastness beyond. Not only has He called into existence that which was not, but He maintains its existence continually: 'For in him we live, and move, and have our being' (Acts 17: 28).

God's Sovereignty in Creation

In creating the world, with supreme dignity He comands substance to materialise by the very simplicity of His Word. He clothes the world with fertility in land and sea and sky. He crowns His creation with Adam and Eve, the first human beings. 'In the beginning God created the heaven and the earth. And the earth was without form, and void; and darkness was upon the face of the deep. And the Spirit of God moved upon the face of the waters. And God said, Let there be light... And the Lord God formed man of the dust of the ground, and breathed into his nostrils the breath of life; and man became a living soul' (Gen. 1:1-3; 2:7). This was the very breath of God, and man could henceforth never be truly satisfied with anything less than God Himself, the source and centre of his being.

So great is the God who created our world, and all that exists in the galaxies of endless and limitless space, that we stand trembling at the thought of such greatness. Not only is He the creator and the upholder of all things, but He is also supreme and perfect in His every attribute. Indeed, when we have said all, we have not even begun to penetrate the dimensions and qualities that are beyond our imaginings; let alone our comprehension. Before such a God we are lost in wonder, love and praise.

God's Sovereignty in the Affairs of Men

In all His dealings with the children of men, and in all that He undertakes to do in His divine plan of redemption, this God is sovereign in the full and free expression of His will. When we are confronted with the will of God, our decisions fade into insignificance, our clamouring voices and the dictates of our hearts have to bend to the absolute will of God.

Men have always delighted in power, and greedily grasp from one another any opportunity given to seize more. Men and nations, swollen with pride in their abilities, strive for authority that can send others hither and thither at their whim. But God is omnipotent, and when He commands all must obey. All power belongs to Him, the power that holds countless galaxies in the palm of His hand, and the power that sustains and cares for the sparrow. Our Lord Jesus Christ, standing before Pilate in the courtroom, reminded him that he would have no power at all, were it not given him from above. Men have imagined that they are mighty, and have gathered their forces to achieve some selfish end; but God in the twinkling of an eye has so moved that all is changed and their plans frustrated.

God's Sovereign Rule of His People

This is exemplified many times over in the long and arduous history of the children of Israel. We realise that their destiny is in the hands of a greater power than the particular empire that held sway over them at the time. It often seemed as if the Jewish nation would be swallowed up in the affairs of the greater nations towering around her. And so she would have, but for the intervention of God, proving again and again His supremacy in the affairs of men, as He continued to deal in mercy with this tiny country and to unfold His plan for her.

There are many incidents in the history of the Jews which illustrate the principle of God's overruling care. In the time of King Jehoshaphat, for example, news comes to the king of many armies from far and near mercilessly bearing down upon the little nation. A general assembly is called, and the king seeks the face of God. His prayer is both moving and profound. He remembers the attributes of God: 'O Lord God of our fathers, art not thou God in heaven? and rulest not thou over all the kingdoms of the heathen? and in thine hand is there not power and might, so that none is able to withstand thee?' (2 Chron. 20:6). He then reminds God of His promises to Abraham, and His faithful fulfilment of these thus far. Finally, he sums up the present desperate situation, and ends with the telling phrase, 'our eyes are upon thee' (2 Chron. 20:12).

God is swift to reply. He is still the God of

Israel. His purposes and promises are unchanging, His abilities undiminished and His care for them constant. The word that came was consistent with a God who is supreme and in full control. 'Be not afraid nor dismayed by reason of this great multitude; for the battle is not yours but God's... Ye shall not need to fight in this battle: set yourselves, stand ye still, and see the salvation of the Lord with you, O Judah and Jerusalem: fear not, nor be dismayed; tomorrow go out against them: for the Lord will be with you' (2 Chron. 20:15,17). The king and the people are overwhelmed with the might and majesty of God: 'And Jehoshaphat bowed his head with his face to the ground: and all Judah and the inhabitants of Jerusalem fell before the Lord, worshipping the Lord... And when they began to sing and to praise, the Lord set ambushments against the children of Ammon, Moab, and Mount Seir... and they were smitten' (2 Chron. 20:18,22).

On another occasion we note that God uses the might of Nebuchadnezzar and other enemy forces to punish Israel for doing 'that which was evil in the sight of the Lord' (2 Kings 24:1,4).

God's All-Embracing Sovereignty

We learn from these and similar events that everything is in the hand of God, and we begin to see that all things work for God's ultimate purpose. Sometimes His hand is clearly seen, whilst at other times what takes place remains a mystery to our understanding. The supreme example of this is the crucifixion of our Saviour. Men schemed against the Lord in their hatred, seized Him, and nailed Him to the cross. Men sought to do their utmost against the Christ, but God had planned in eternity that it should be so. The Saviour knew that His hour was to come, and recognised it when it came. God's eternal plan was revealed and carried through in due time. We see here the full responsibility of men for their individual actions, and the violent opposition of evil powers; but at the same time we see here the unfrustrated accomplishing of God's purposes.

At all times, in all events, He is sovereign. 'So it must be concluded that while the turbulent state of the world deprives *us* of judgment, God by the pure light of His own righteousness and wisdom regulates these very commotions in the most exact order and directs them to their proper end' (John Calvin).

This God is sovereign in all His creation, in all the affairs of mankind, in salvation, and also in the life of His Church. In the long history of the Christian Church there have been factors militating against her, causing great dismay to the believers, and yet these very same events have ultimately been used to fulfil the purposes of God. In times of dreadful persecution and suffering, and in the midst of sorrows, the people of God have been enriched, the Church purified, and many added to the Faith. In such circumstances and at such times the Church has become powerful. Does this not prove to us that the gates of hell shall not prevail against the true Church, because it is His? And how humbling it is to remember that the sovereign concern of God is not only for the Church as a body, but for every individual believer in that body.

2. How this Truth affects us

Pride is Humbled

To understand the truth of God's supremacy is literally impossible for us as natural men, because our pride in our abilities and achievements, coupled with our limitations as finite creatures, prevent us from ever admitting anyone to be greater than ourselves. Added to this is the fact that our minds are darkened by Satan. We are thus totally incapable of any kind of response to the things of God. But when we are quickened by the grace of God, and brought into a right relationship with Him through a saving experience of the Lord Jesus Christ, then the 'eyes of our understanding' are enlightened. He takes away the dimness which veils our minds, and grants us a sight greater and more startling than the sight granted to the eyes of blind Bartimaeus. It is then that we begin to understand the deep things of God. True wisdom and knowledge consists in knowing that there is none greater than the God of Abraham, Isaac and Jacob, who is also the Father of our Lord Jesus Christ. 'The fear of the Lord is the beginning of knowledge: but fools despise wisdom and instruction' (Prov. 1:7).

This knowledge in our hearts and minds is very precious to us. It is given to us as God Himself touches our thinking, enabling us to see with clarity that which previously we could barely discern. The recognition of this fact alone is a startling event in the human heart and mind. The very fact that we admit a superior, supernatural power, above and infinitely greater than ourselves, is in itself an important landmark. To acknowledge that God is supreme humbles us, as our pride instinctively rebels against the knowledge that there is a limit to our abilities, and that in the spiritual realm we are totally incapable, unless God enlightens and empowers us.

True Understanding

The knowledge that God is sovereign changes both our attitude to life and our understanding and evaluation of the events that take place. Now we know that He is God, and that what oftentimes seems to be confusion can in fact never be out of His control. He begins a work with the full intention of completing and perfecting it. Seeing that we are in the hands of such a God, 'we know that all things work together for good to them that love God, to them who are the called according to His purpose' (Rom. 8:28). We will also perhaps begin to realise that in order to achieve this end God must surely at times move 'in a mysterious way, His wonders to perform'.

Increased Trust in God

Our lives are henceforth to be lived in a different light, in a new way, not leaning upon our own understanding, but looking to and trusting in God. Recognising that our own comprehension is limited, and convinced of God's supremacy, we now seek His wisdom. This is not as easy as it may seem, for we have considerable confidence in our own ability to think things out, and we still tend to delight in solving our problems unaided. We need to be reminded that we are not the master of every situation, nor the controller of our future. It is no ordinary man who seeks the guidance of God, and devotes his energies to applying God's counsel to his own daily life.

Indeed, the Christian has a depth of understanding of life itself that he could never have appreciated on his own. He is like a person made alive to another dimension. No understanding of history is complete if its Planner is left out, and no philosophy of life is adequate if the Creator of life is ignored. To understand the meaning of existence in any real measure we must know God Himself.

Deep Comfort

The knowledge that God is sovereign is also a very encouraging thing. We know that the immortal God *rules* in our lives, and that our present and our future are in His almighty hand. Surely the knowledge of this is a deep comfort to the soul, that the invisible and wise God cares for us! All that we care about and desire comes under the sway of His infinite knowledge and ability. This knowledge warms our hearts, and true adoration towards our Lord fills our whole being. We worship Him as our hearts are overwhelmed with the majesty of the King of Glory, and with the assurance that He reigns in our hearts. As we embrace the truth in this way, a new reality is brought into our lives. A miracle has taken place. We have seen and understood. 'God be thanked, that ye were the servants of sin, but ye have obeyed from the heart that form of doctrine which was delivered you' (Rom. 6:17). This is more than an intellectual assent to a great doctrine, though even that can evoke submission to His great supremacy. It is a reception with mind and heart, which has its outworking in our lives, of a truth and of a God who is gloriously sovereign, who reigns in us, bringing glory to Himself.

Peace in Life's Storms

How will all this affect our lives, as we are thrown out into the turmoil of our daily circumstances? The believer, as he increasingly learns to discern the sovereignty of God in the events of his life, finds that he is secure. We are all aware of the events that sometimes rush upon us like an angry storm, when our hearts would almost fail within us. If our trust is in God and His absolute sovereignty, we will not despair. Our reliance will be, not upon the present circumstances and their immediate outcome, but upon God Himself.

When the disciples found themselves in a storm at sea, fear gripped their hearts, for they were afraid of the angry waves and the raging of the wind. In their fear they rebuked the Saviour for His apparent unconcern for them: 'Master, carest thou not that we perish?' The Lord expressed amazement at their attitude. Were they not aware that the Master of all the universe and the Lord of creation was in the ship? How was it that they feared the elements? He turned and chided them, 'O ye of little faith'. Nevertheless, He silenced the storm, stilling the tempest and the fury of the sea, whilst they looked on with trembling hearts and reverential fear, realising with awe who it was that sailed with them in their little ship.

Contentment in Circumstances

Surely we also have known that He is in our circumstances, that our Lord never slumbers or sleeps. The knowledge that these billows of circumstances cannot match their strength against His power is a deep comfort to our hearts. We must believe in God in this way, believing in His divine purposes, in His care for His own. We must believe without flinching, like Job who in the midst of all his trouble cried out in faith, 'Oh that my words were now written! Oh that they were printed in a book! That they were graven with an iron pen and lead in the rock for ever! For I know that my redeemer liveth, and that he shall stand at the latter day upon the earth' (Job 19:23-25). However destitute we may be in the circumstances of our life, however much driven to despair, we must not leave God out of the situation. We must learn to believe that His purposes cannot be frustrated, that the ultimate good that He promises to His own will be realised, because He is sovereign.

Purposeful Living

Each day takes on a new meaning, as with true heartfelt obedience we look to the Lord, and to the unfolding of His sovereign will for us. Life loses its aimless character; the daily task and common round become part of something infinitely greater. Wherever we are placed or led, we now seek to know the purpose of God for our lives, for He has a definite purpose for each of His people. 'For we are his workmanship, created in Christ Jesus unto good works, which God hath before ordained that we should walk in them' (Eph. 2:10). Events take on a new meaning as we become increasingly aware that He is working out His purpose in us, preparing and moulding us to conform to the pattern that He has willed.

He is Lord of all; He rules in every part of His creation in absolute wisdom, and He rules in our hearts and lives, for He is our Sovereign. He is worthy of our trust. Our future is safe in His almighty hand. The God that we believe in is supreme in creation, in the events of history, in the affairs of the Church, and in our own individual lives. 'Thine, O Lord, is the greatness, and the power, and the glory, and the victory, and the majesty: for all that is in the heaven and in the earth is thine; thine is the kingdom, O Lord, and thou art exalted as head above all' (1 Chron. 29:11).

Ye fearful saints, fresh courage take;
The clouds ye so much dread
Are big with mercy, and shall break
In blessings on your head.

3

THE CHOICE

Election! This biblical word can bring joy to the heart of the believer, and yet to some it brings resentment, if not firm rejection. What is our response when we see or hear this word? I remember being present at a Bible study once, and when we were confronted with the teaching of election, the leader saying somewhat faintheartedly 'We won't stay with controversial subjects!' But since this teaching is in the Bible, can we afford to ignore it, and then one day have to face its Author? We must treat the Word of God with deep reverence, and seek His aid when we find difficulty in understanding it. Surely, when we consider the greatness of our God, His infinite and boundless abilities, His glorious attributes, who are we to question His ways?

1. The Truth about Election

The meaning of election

Let us begin by saying just what we mean by the word 'election', and then set it in its Biblical context. I remember once, whilst appreciating and enjoying a painting by one of the masters, the thought of God's eternal plan came to me. There in the foreground stood the figures, painted with bold strokes and vivid colours; yet how strange and unnatural they would have appeared if there had been nothing else on the canvas. Filling the canvas were the gentle background colours of mauves, browns and their many different blends. Without them the portrait would have been unreal. In some strange way they held the whole together, gentle and unobtrusive, and yet essential to the painting.

Similarly, in the foreground of our consciousness are the events and circumstances, the decisions and responses that fill our lives. It appears that we have a major part to play; the colours are bold and clear. Yet on consideration we can see the contribution made by factors outside ourselves, and gradually in our thinking the background colours of the canvas fill in. Slowly we begin to see the guiding of a hand infinitely greater than our own, and eventually we realise that it was God who planned it all. The truth of salvation, and of our part in it, stands out clearly in our immediate experience. But on consideration we become increasingly aware of a sovereign God predestinating and electing a people to His own glory, and of His eternal purposes as mighty mountains of grace giving strength to the ground on which we stand.

'Election may be defined as that eternal act of God whereby He, in His sovereign good pleasure, and on account of no foreseen merit in them, chooses a certain number of men to be the recipients of special grace and of eternal salvation' (Berkhof). 'And we know that all things work together for good to them that love God, to them who are the called according to his purpose. For whom he did foreknow, he also did predestinate to be conformed to the image of his Son, that he might be the first-born among many brethren. Moreover, whom he did predestinate, them he also called: and whom he called, them he also justified: and whom he justified, them he also glorified' (Rom. 8:28-30).

God's action in electing

The Lord Jesus Christ, in His great prayer recorded in John 17, unfolds to us something of the wonder of God's election. We see His love and care for His children; we are given a glimpse of His purposes in gathering His own: 'I have manifested thy name unto the men which thou gavest me out of the world: thine they were, and thou gavest them me; and they have kept thy word' (John 17:6). We know that the Bible speaks of the election of the nation of Israel for a special purpose, and the election of individuals out of that nation for particular tasks which God had for them. But we are thinking of election here with particular reference to God's choice of people to be heirs of eternal life – 'For many are called, but few are chosen' (Matt. 22:14).

We readily acknowledge and respect our own choice in all that we do – the friends we have chosen, the career we have selected, the decisions we have made in crucial times – and *we* are fallible! We have been willing to abide by the decision and choice of others, from the captain's choice of his team at school to the decisions of a government with respect to nations. These things we accept, despite the fact that men, though sincere, are fallible. How strange it is that deep pride and prejudice of heart causes us to resent the choice of One whose ways and judgments are infallible!

Election must not be viewed in isolation

In endeavouring to understand election, perhaps we ought to remember that election itself must not be held up on its own, as it were, for display. It will appear cold, impersonal, unrelated, unreal, and our longing hearts will chill with fear at the seeming indifference of such a teaching. We know in everyday experience that when we have heard of some remarkable event, much has depended upon accompanying factors.

Let us suppose that someone has made a very strong statement which we find alarming. On enquiry we find that the statement was made by someone for whom we have profound respect, whose character and judgment we do not question. That being so, our considered response will be that although we do not fully understand why the statement was made, we nevertheless still accept that it was made with some good and sufficient reason. And we would hold to this because we trust the person. Our sovereign God is perfect in Himself, infinitely wise and good, and in Him is no error or carelessness. Since it is such a God who elects, then deep in our hearts we can trust His mercy and His grace, knowing that 'He hath done all things well'. There is no fickleness, unreliability or vindictiveness in Him. These things belong to men. His choice is like Himself, supreme, perfect and good.

Election exalts the glory of God's grace

When we consider election, we learn to appreciate far more the glorious truth that our salvation is truly by the grace of God, and not by any merit of our own. It brings to us the knowledge that our salvation rests on something far greater than our own response to the gospel of our Saviour. For our God is unchangeable; His will is unalterable. The hand of God upon us draws us to Himself, with a strange compulsion stronger than our rebellion and disobedience. In the salvation wrought by the Lord Jesus Christ we are accepted, given grace to persevere to the end, and finally brought to Himself in glory: 'Nevertheless the foundation of God standeth sure, having this seal, The Lord knoweth them that are his' (2 Tim. 2:19).

Thus, although we can look back happily to a time in our lives when we were brought by the mercy of God to see our need, and then to a knowledge of salvation in the merits of the Lord Jesus Christ, we also realise that there is more to all this than a date. The seal has two dates. One is the time when we were turned to God; the other bears the stamp of eternity – 'According as he hath chosen us in him before the foundation of the world' (Eph. 1:4).

Election is unconditional

The election of God is unconditional. There is *no* merit – not even a faith which is our own making – that we are able to offer Him as some vague prerequisite to salvation. The forgiven sinner will always be amazed that God looked upon him and had mercy. The grace of God to such a one is irresistible. The sound of the gospel is sweet to our hearing and blessed to our hearts, for it speaks to us of the love and the call of the Father. Although we cannot understand why He called us to Him, yet we know that He is just and holy in all His ways, and we cannot but worship Him. 'As it is written, Jacob have I loved, but Esau have I hated. What shall we say then? Is there unrighteousness with God? God forbid. For he saith to Moses, I will have mercy on whom I will have mercy, and I will have compassion on whom I will have compassion' (Rom. 9:13-15).

Election is often misrepresented

How often, when we are angry, have we caricatured a person or a cause in order to arouse sympathy for our own position, little realising that our very attitude has betrayed our own failing! Men have often misrepresented the teaching of election, imputing to it the notion that men must be robots, or that God is cruel. This is a grossly unfair assessment. In arriving at such a conclusion they are applying logical arguments to only one aspect of the truth. There is much more to the teachings of God than that which appears on the surface. Scripture *does* emphasise man's obedience, and responsibility; it addresses itself to our hearts, minds and wills. But let us also remember with reverence that God is supreme in all things. Let us not be so surprised that there is a wisdom above our own, a hand unseen that guides, and a choice that is infallible because it is His.

2. How this Truth affects us

Joy

To belong to the people of God is in itself a joy to which nothing in this world can be compared. We belong to Him, and experience the joy of knowing that it was the God of all creation who sought our souls: 'Henceforth I call you not servants; for the servant knoweth not what his Lord doeth: but I have called you friends; for all things that I have heard of my Father I have made known unto you. Ye have not chosen me, but I have chosen you, and ordained you, that ye should go and bring forth fruit, and that your fruit should remain' (John 15:15,16). Something of the wonder of this privilege dawns on our souls as we read such words.

There begins to grow in us the realisation of an assurance and a security that no one is able to shake.

Assurance

I've found a Friend; O such a Friend,
He loved me ere I knew Him;
He drew me with the cords of love,
And thus He bound me to Him;
And round my heart still closely twine
Those ties which nought can sever,
For I am His, and He is mine,
For ever and for ever.

With all the assurance that this brings, we know that our salvation is not dependent upon our feelings, but upon God's will. With such knowledge, even when Satan assails us with fearful doubts as to whether there has been a work of grace in our hearts, we rest upon God's immutable will. Those whom the Father has chosen in Christ from eternity will come to the Saviour, and can never be separated from the Lord.

Delight in God

In days of gross ungodliness and sin, there still remains on this earth a people of God. Yet how easy it is to conform to the ways of men. Let us consider the relationship that we are in: chosen of God, redeemed by the blood of the Lord Jesus Christ to belong to Him, the eternal God. Our hearts warm towards Him; our minds delight in the knowledge of Him and it is then that marks of the elect are seen in us increasingly. The grace of God becomes yet more evident in our lives. 'Wherefore the rather, brethren, give diligence to make your calling and election sure: for if ye do these things, ye shall never fall' (2 Pet. 1:10).

Walking with God

Each day we live is a day granted to us by God's mercy. He alone knows the length of our life, and what He has in view for our ultimate good. We enter each new day with the solemn knowledge within us that we are His. This knowledge should not estrange us from others, however, causing unhappiness and sorrow to those with whom we have to do. It is not by telling others that we are different; but rather, by the grace and loveliness of His work in us, that men should become conscious of the fact that we belong to Him. Peter and John stood out amongst other men for this – 'and they took knowledge of them, that they had been with Jesus' (Acts 4:13). Because we are the Lord's we do not need to spend our time convincing others in an aggressive way.

When we have a firm and quiet assurance in our hearts that we are His, and are able rightly to divide the word of truth, we can afford to be calm and to take opportunities when God gives them to us. It is the man who is unsure of himself that must be constantly fighting, constantly asserting himself. We can afford to be patient and to be calm in our spirit, because we know that our times are in God's hands. We seek out His will, with a firm resolution to perform it and know no panic when opposition confronts us: 'If God be for us, who can be against us?' (Rom. 8:31).

Making our election sure

We must not allow ourselves, however, to be apathetic and indifferent to the path of good works that lies before us. Recognising that there is much to be learnt, much to be achieved, the Christian must be active in making his calling and election sure, in confirming through the quality of his life, the profound and avowed conviction of his heart. He must see to it that he does not neglect the means of grace. He must be vigorous in the application of the will of God to his life. He must be willing to learn and respond in true obedience to all the demands of his Lord. If we are not thus occupied, we can be well assured that we are not showing the signs of spiritual life that are to be expected in the elect of God.

Joyful obedience

Added to an obedient life there is also the joy of seeking and doing the will of God. There is an element of excitement as we embark upon a day which we know is in His hand, knowing that our highest and truest happiness is to abide in His will and to perform what He would have us do. Even when opposition mounts because of our witness, we are not dismayed, because we know that we are His. It was H G Spafford who, on receiving news of the death of his daughters the same day that he had also been informed of the total collapse of the Bank that held all his money, quietly turned to the Lord, and inspired by Him wrote these words:

> When peace like a river attendeth my way,
> When sorrows like sea-billows roll;
> Whatever my lot, Thou hast taught me to say:
> It is well, it is well with my soul!

Urgent witnessing

We are also called to be witnesses, and are commanded to preach the gospel of salvation. We now have a new urgency. No longer is it a vague command to go to people for whom we may have no natural feeling because they are strangers. We are now seeking the as yet unconverted members of our already predestinated spiritual family.

In my early ministry I had the privilege of knowing the sister of Evan Roberts who was remarkably used of God in the Welsh Revival of 1904. She recounted an occasion when she was serving as a missionary in Africa in the early years of the twentieth century. The chief of the tribe had died, and, as was the tribal custom, that night he was to be buried together with his wives and all his servants. In the stillness of the night the missionaries were only too painfully aware of the sad procession of frightened natives, going to their execution and burial somewhere in the heart of the jungle. Suddenly the stillness was broken by a girl breaking into the missionary compound. She was one of the chief's servants who had escaped, facing the peril of the jungle and fighting her way to the safety of the missionaries' home. At first she was very distraught, but eventually she quietened down, being assured of her safety. Then suddenly she jumped to her feet and gave a heart-rending scream. 'O my brother, O my brother!' Her younger brother was one of the serving-men of the chief's family, and so was being executed with the others. The urgency of this cry inspired the missionaries to an even more urgent pursuit of preaching the gospel, and bringing spiritual brothers and sisters still in darkness and peril to salvation.

God has ordained that they should hear by the word of preaching, and has given to us the responsibility of bearing the news. We are looking for our brothers and sisters. We should pray for the effective preaching of the Word, so that those still in darkness may be brought into light. 'How then shall they call on him in whom they have not believed? and how shall they believe in him of whom they have not heard? and how shall they hear without a preacher? And how shall they preach, except they be sent? as it is written, How beautiful are the feet of them that preach the gospel of peace, and bring glad tidings of good things!' (Rom. 10:14,15).

4

THE PROBLEM

I can remember when I was a child hearing a story that I have not been able to forget. I believe that this was because the story told me a truth about myself. It was about a little boy who asked his father if he could go out for a swim after lunch. His father replied that he was to wait until later, when the family would be going together, but meanwhile he could go for a walk if he wished. A little later, the father saw the boy pass his room, carrying a towel and a swimming suit. When asked to account for this, the boy assured his father that he did not intend to swim; he was simply taking his swimming suit along in case he might be tempted. Even as a child, I understood the mind of a boy who behaved like that.

1. The Truth about Sin

Recognising sin

It does not take us long to discover a certain truth about ourselves. Sadly we learn to recognise that there is within us a fault which is more than an inclination to be a little deceptive. As we go on in years, what seemed at first to be a little defect becomes increasingly apparent. There is a bias in us. We find it easier to criticise than to praise, to condemn than to encourage, to choose that which is to our own advantage than to be unselfish in our actions.

Slowly we observe in the world around us that this fault runs through the whole of society. Men will deceive in order to gain, and will kill in order to dominate. The history of the world is a story of warfare, a story of man's inhumanity to man. Of course, there *is* good, but it has to struggle for survival in a world of scheming men, with their hearts and imaginations inclined towards evil. We *are* sinners, and because of this we sin.

I suppose that one of the hardest truths for man to acknowledge is his sinfulness before God. This affects his thinking, his actions, and ultimately his achievements. Yet, distasteful as it may be to our human pride, we will make no progress in our spiritual pilgrimage until this lesson is learnt, and our hearts are convinced of its truth.

Sin's depths

The Scripture are emphatic that man in his natural state is dead in trespasses and sins. A clear diagnosis of a patient's complaint is essential before any remedy can be applied. We readily give assent to accuracy and honesty in every other realm of human activity. Sadly, in the realm where it matters most of all we are vague and evasive.

The teaching in the Bible on the depravity of the human heart, however, is abundantly clear. 'All have sinned, and come short of the glory of God' (Rom. 3:23). A vivid and sorrowful picture of the state of our hearts and minds is given in the letter to the Ephesians, when Paul reminds the Christians that their way of life should be different now: 'This I say therefore, and testify in the Lord, that ye henceforth walk not as other Gentiles walk, in the vanity of their mind, having the understanding darkened, being alienated from the life of God through the ignorance that is in them, because of the blindness of their heart' (Eph. 4:17,18). We can gather from such verses that the trouble is deep-seated. This is no superficial description and assessment of man's condition. It is not something that can be remedied by a little effort on his part. There is blindness in his mind, and his heart is stubbornly alienated from God.

Sin's origins

Why do we sin? How is it that we lean so readily towards that which is wrong, and run so easily with the course of this world? We are told in the book of Genesis of our early beginnings, of how God created man in His own image, and provided him with a partner. Into this garden of happiness and life Satan entered, tempting the woman, who in turn beguiled the man. When man fell into sin he was immediately separated from God, who drove him out of the garden. His innocent nakedness became shameful exposure, and we read of Adam's efforts to hide from the presence of God. The condemnation of God is clearly delivered: 'Because thou hast hearkened unto the voice of thy wife, and hast eaten of the tree, of which I commanded thee, saying, Thou shalt not eat of it: cursed is the ground for thy sake; in sorrow shalt thou eat of it all the days of thy life; Thorns also and thistles shall it bring forth to thee; and thou shalt eat the herb of the field; In the sweat of thy face shalt thou eat bread, till thou return unto the ground; for out of it wast thou taken: for dust thou art, and unto dust shalt thou return' (Gen. 3:17-19).

Sin's extent

From this we learn of the total depravity of man – not that we are entirely evil, and incapable of any good, but that all we do is coloured by sin. This impurity shows itself to a greater or lesser degree in everything we undertake. It is always there. Our minds are darkened and our wills enslaved by sin: 'For I know that in me (that is, in my flesh) dwelleth no good thing: for to will is present with me; but how to perform that which is good I find not' (Rom. 7:18). With this bias towards sin, our thinking is inclined towards that which is sinful, our main aim in life is the gratification of self. It would be foolish to say that there is no good in us, and that all we do is unclean. By the operation of common grace man is capable of civil good, good behaviour, and even good religious aspiration; but he is totally incapable of spiritual good without the saving grace of God.

Sin's inward character

There are, and have been, many men who have lived apparently unselfish and sacrificial lives in the service of others, just as there are also men who have given themselves over to the hatred and ruin of others. What about these finer and nobler examples of manhood that we sometimes see? Are they also sinful?

It is important for us to realise the nature of sin. We are inclined to think of it only in terms of specific failings in outward behaviour. Every malady, however, does not produce a rash so that all may see the evidence of the disease. And yet a person can be equally sick, although there may be very little outward evidence. The Pharisees had a superficial view of holiness and sin, believing that if they kept certain observances and avoided open sin they were blameless. Our Lord, however, exposes their shallowness, and showed them that sin was something inward: 'Ye have heard that it was said by them of old time, Thou shalt not commit adultery: But I say unto you, that whosoever looketh on a woman to lust after her hath committed adultery with her already in his heart' (Matt. 5:27,28). This opens a new realm that we had never thought of – one that concerns the motives of our hearts and the wanderings of our minds.

Who then can escape such a standard? Even the most virtuous stands condemned, and bears out the Scriptural truth that 'The heart is deceitful above all things, and desperately wicked: who can know it?' (Jer. 17:9). The Bible does not hide from us, nor spare us from hearing the truth about ourselves: 'the Lord seeth not as man seeth; for man looketh on the outward appearance, but the Lord looketh on the heart' (1 Sam. 16:7).

Sinners by nature

Sin dwells in the centre of man's being, that is, in his heart, and because of this man's whole personality – intellect, will and affections – is affected by it. Our hard and impenitent hearts are strangers to the love of God. Despite the mind and the intellect which man has been given, he is incapable of choosing God. Man is a sinner by nature, a truth which he sadly confirms daily by the way that he lives. As God turns our hearts and minds to seek after salvation, it is essential that we recognise our desperate need. We have broken the law of God, we are alienated from Him; we stand condemned in His sight. If we are to be saved, there must needs be an act of mercy by which God approaches the helpless sinner, granting him even the listening ear and a receptive heart, so that he might hear and obey His call.

2. Effects of Salvation from Sin

Forgiveness of sins

Now let us consider the man who has come to a saving knowledge of the Lord Jesus Christ. Because of the penalty paid for sin on Calvary by His Saviour, his sins are forgiven. He is pardoned. He is free from the bondage and the consequences of his sin. The question now arises, has he finished with sin? Although his guilt has been removed and the power of sin is broken, there yet remains in him another principle warring against the soul. He must be fully aware of this fact, and face the grim reality of a race to be run, a fight to be fought. When a man has then known of the grace of God in salvation, and is elated by the wonder and joy of it all, it is good and wise for him to be reminded of the humble stock from which he came. When we have tasted and seen that the Lord is good, when we have known what it means to be a forgiven person and a recipient of the grace of God, let us not forget the miry pit from which we were delivered. Having known the mercy of God in redemption do we not forget so easily the price that was paid as a penalty for our sin? Should we not be increasingly aware of the holiness and the righteousness of God?

Sin's power broken yet its principle remains

The pardoned sinner can rejoice that the penalty for his sin has been fully paid, and that its power has been broken in his life: yet he has to learn that as a believer he still has to contend with the principle of sin that is in him.

At first, maybe, the words of Scripture seem strange to our ears, when we hear the anguished cry of Paul, 'O wretched man that I am! who shall deliver me from the body of this death?' (Rom. 7:24); or when perhaps we read of King David, who had to come to the Lord for restoration, having repented of his sin, and having learnt through this experience something more of the requirements of God: 'The sacrifices of God are a broken spirit: a broken and a contrite heart, O God, thou wilt not despise' (Ps. 51:17). But we need to recognise full well the depravity of the human heart. This knowledge needs to be driven deep into our being, so that we may know, as an irrefutable fact about ourselves, that 'in me dwelleth no good thing'. It is important for us to be under no misapprehension regarding ourselves, for how readily our old nature will arrogantly raise its broken head, in an endeavour to re-establish itself. As we become more aware of our unworthiness, we are moved to repentance; we see our sin as an offence against God, and we seek to turn from it in abhorrence.

Hatred of sin

While it is humbling to learn this about ourselves, it can also be a most blessed experience. We begin to discover more and more of the meaning of our Lord's phrase in the Sermon on the Mount: 'Blessed are they that mourn: for they shall be comforted' (Matt. 5:4). If we would seek the comfort that comes from Him, filling our hearts with joy and praise, then we must learn to hate the sin that is within us. We need to mourn, to grieve, and to depart from our sin, and yet at the same time to be upheld by the comfort of God, as we grow in grace and in the knowledge of Him.

Falling into sin

As we learn what it is to be exercised by God's grace – sometimes being painfully weaned from besetting sins, at other times learning more of positive obedience to His will – we slowly begin to realise that true godliness is a costly business.

I wonder how far we are willing to go in our spiritual lives? Is it not true that the picture we see in the Song of Solomon is only too often true of ourselves? In it we find the woman lying indifferently on her couch, content to keep her lover on the other side of the door at her beck and call while he occasionally clicks the latch as a reminder that he is there. Then, alas, the dreadful realisation dawns upon her that he has withdrawn, and is no longer waiting upon her. Desperately she seeks him, remembering his beauty as the fairest of all. So often we have kept the Saviour thus, only to feel the chill in our souls, and to find the blessedness we once knew rapidly fading. Our cold hearts and unbending wills keep Him outside the door. The sweet fellowship is broken. No longer is there joy in the reading of His word, in prayer and the singing of His praises. What have we done? We have forgotten our need, we have neglected the means of grace, and we have turned aside. We need to be constantly reminded that we were dead, and He has made us alive; that we were unclean, and He has washed us; that we were strangers, and He has made us His own.

Realising our sinfulness

We live in a busy and a troubled world, competitive and cruel. Gone is the simple life that we mistakenly but romantically believe our forefathers led, free from the anxieties, the pressures and temptations of this present evil world. But we have to face the fact that we live *now*, and that every age would have preferred another, believing the pastures to be greener and the hills gentler in some other place at some other time. Every man has to live the Christian life where he finds himself. Our conduct in such a world must be based upon a sure knowledge of the sinfulness of our hearts.

The first thing we need to do is to keep a careful watch upon ourselves, as we can so easily be swept along in the course of this world. The fear of man, the opinion of others, can so easily dominate our thinking. It is easy to remain silent and to pass unnoticed as Christians, lest there should be a conflict of opinion, or, more honestly, lest others might know that we are believers.

We must recognise our weakness here, and put our trust in God and not in ourselves.

Brokenness for sin

What are we like as believers in the company of other people? Are we known for our self-assurance, our assertiveness and spiritual pride? It is so easy to allow the difference between us and those who do not know the Lord to become a barrier over which we smugly view others. So easily do we forget that we are not what we are by our own merit, but by the grace and mercy of God. Let us remember that we are sinners, and recognise that, whatever sin we may see in our fellow human beings, the potential for it is in our own hearts too. Indeed, the sight of sin should drive us, not to despise the sinner who has not yet known of God's mercy, but rather to cry out that we might be more and more delivered from the ways of sin and seek more earnestly the righteousness of God.

The knowledge of our depravity drives us more and more to a knowledge of the grace of God. We become a people who are utterly dependent upon God, who desire to please and obey Him above all else in our lives. I believe that this will lead us to a greater degree of brokenness and contrition. Painful as this may be, it produces a tenderness which is unmistakable. It is the tenderness that is produced by the dealings of God, when He has wounded us sorely in weaning and winning us from our disobedient ways, in order to heal us well, and to restore the bones which He has broken. Strange as it may seem, it is in this school of God's dealings with us that we emerge as a people full of grace and truth in our lives. We need say very little; men will know where we have been. We need not assert our views or display ourselves; it will be known that we are there by a new authority which comes from God. There will be in our attitude to others a sympathy and a compassion, an understanding heart which we could only have received from God Himself and His dealings with us.

[illegible]

[illegible]

[illegible] the school of [illegible] doctrine [illegible]

[illegible]

5

THE NEW CREATURE

How many times down through the centuries has been heard the cry of anguish from the heart of man 'What must I do to be saved?' The jailer whose story is recounted in the book of Acts represents so many who have sought the Lord in distress of heart and in fear.

1. The Gift of Salvation

God's method of awakening

There are times when our ordinary security and comfort is shaken and we realise with dreadful reality our helpless frailty. At such times we are more willing to listen to the voice of God. We are such proud creatures that when all is well, when the present is to our liking and the future apparently secure, we are unapproachable. Our arrogance and self-assurance carry us along, and in our ignorance we foolishly imagine that all will continue as it is. But there are periods in our lives when we pause for a moment and consider our end, and the meaning and purpose of existence. The means which God uses to bring us to Himself vary greatly, but He bides His time before speaking to our hearts. Sometimes death is the occasion, when we are deeply moved and affected by the loss of someone dear to us, and for a while we are compelled to consider our end and our eternal destiny. Not infrequently has He spoken to us in time of sickness, and shown to us our frailty and dependence. There are others who can testify that in sin they became sick of sin, and in desperation they sought the Lord. There are undoubtedly many ways in which He can approach the soul, and appeal to our deepest longing. Sadly, however, we forget so soon, and when the crisis is over the sunshine of indifference shines in our lives again; we forget the storm and the clouds, revelling in the present happiness. God deals with us and eventually we become aware of our need.

Like a stranded sheep

A friend of mine and his wife have a mountain sheep farm and they have written of their dealings with sheep, and the simple and profound lessons learnt. One story described how a sheep had foolishly strayed and found herself in great difficulties. In her desperation she somehow found her way to a perilous ledge high on the rock face from which there seemed no way of escape. How the sheep had found her way there was amazing, but there she was. We need not be so amazed, for we too have found ourselves stranded on the slopes of sin, in impossible situations. However did we arrive there? The sin of our heart found a way. The sheep, on realising her peril began to bleat frantically, endeavouring to attract the attention of the shepherd as he passed by. Strangely, however, he took no notice of her predicament. The following day again he passed by, and by now the sheep was considerably weaker, but roused herself to further strenuous effort at his approach. Again however, he took no notice of her. On the third day, her calls are weak when he approaches. By now the sheep has lost all strength, and her bleating is pitifully faint. Now he climbs down, hauls her helpless form up the rock face, and brings her safely home. Why the delay? If he had gone to her when she first called, her struggles to assist would have sent them both hurtling down the slope. He waited until she was past self-effort and showed that he alone, without assistance or interference, could rescue her. How many have called upon the Lord to begin with, perhaps more for attention than for anything else, vaguely acknowledging their danger, but still believing that a combined effort or a little help is all that is necessary. He will pass by, not unheeding, but knowing the right time is not yet. But there comes that time in our lives when the cry is from the heart. We have lost all confidence in ourselves, all trust in our vain efforts, and we cry for mercy. He will not refuse the soul that calls for help. He will come to lift us out of our sin and despair, and carry us home. He is the good Shepherd.

Nothing in my hand I bring,
Simply to Thy cross I cling.

Awareness of our needs

It is a hard task to bring many of us to listen to His voice, and yet once heard it cannot be forgotten. We may have heard the gospel many times, and yet on that day when we heard with understanding it seemed as if we were hearing for the first time. To have dealings with God will always be a searching experience. There are no half-measures; there is no superficial covering over or patching up, but one which involves us to the very depth of our being. We need to be made new creatures by the regenerating power of the Holy Spirit.

When God approaches us, we become to some extent aware of what He is, and thereby of what we are ourselves. The beauty of His holiness, the majesty of His person become increasingly vivid to our consciousness. We realise as never before that He alone is God, reigning supreme in splendour beyond our comprehension, that He is the Creator of all that is. When such a God draws near, we are overwhelmed by a sense of our unworthiness. We realise again and again that we are sinners, and estranged from God because of this dreadful curse. Sin is embedded in our hearts and carved deeply in our minds; it dominates our wills and manifests itself in all our actions. There is no man who can give us the remedy or encourage us by his example. The Scriptures are true, and they tell us 'As it is written, There is none righteous, no, no not one' (Rom. 3:10).

O, how shall I, whose native sphere
Is dark, whose mind is dim,
Before the Ineffable appear,
And on my naked spirit bear
The uncreated beam?

It is no easy task for us to be convinced of this major defect in ourselves. Indeed such is our blindness that even this has to be revealed to us by the Holy Spirit. When at last we are convinced of this truth, we then become painfully aware of our uncleanness in the sight of a God who is holy and pure: 'Thou art of purer eyes than to behold evil, and canst not look on iniquity' (Hab. 1:13).

The terrifying reality that God is pure fills our hearts with dismay. There is no possibility of our sin being bypassed, no hope at all of slipping by and escaping His notice.

Awareness of our danger

The realisation that we are unacceptable because of our sin comes as something of a shock to us. But Scripture has more to say about our sin and what we deserve: 'For the wages of sin is death' (Rom. 6:23). What a dreadful consequence, to be finally rejected! It is the Saviour Himself who said 'Depart from me, ye cursed, into everlasting fire' (Matt. 25:41). What can we do to be saved from such an end? We are already aware that we must die physically, as a consequence of the Fall, but if we are without Christ we are also faced with the grim reality of the second and final death, when we will be condemned by God for ever. 'It is appointed unto men once to die, but after this the judgment' (Heb. 9:27). As we are quickened by God and our understanding enlightened by the Holy Spirit, it is then that we begin to realise the terror of these things; and also to understand the mercy of God.

A new and living way

Salvation is a work of God from beginning to end. It displays the mercy, the grace, and the love of our God. This salvation is complete, effective and acceptable in the sight of Almighty God. All that the Lord did meets with the approval of His Father, because He fulfilled the requirements of the law, both in the letter and in the spirit. We have the Father's own confirmation of this on the occasion of our Lord's baptism: 'And, lo, a voice from heaven, saying, This is my beloved Son, in whom I am well pleased' (Matt. 3:17). At His death on Calvary, when He was nailed to the cross, it is as if time stood still. Cruel and wicked men schemed to destroy Him, Judas with an evil heart betrayed Him, and soldiers in callous obedience nailed Him there. Yet who is without guilt? 'But he was wounded for our transgressions, he was bruised for our iniquities: the chastisement of our peace was upon him; and with his stripes we are healed' (Isa. 53:5). Why did *He* die? Because our punishment is more than *we* can bear. The punishment is death. It is separation from God. It is everlasting torment. What mercy and love is this; that He takes our sin upon Himself and dies for us, paying the penalty for our sin! The pure justice of God is satisfied in the death of His only begotten Son, whose blood is shed for our redemption. By His death at Calvary the Lord Jesus Christ is punished in the sinner's place.

A new principle

A miracle has happened in us. A new principle of spiritual life has been implanted in us, so that the whole direction of our lives from now on is towards God. This is amazing grace indeed. The actual life giving and quickening by God is instantaneous. This is so whether our experience is sudden or over a period of time. This change is performed by God in man's innermost being. It can be described as an invisible but powerful work of God within us. It will not be long however, before the effects of this new life will be felt, and finally manifested in our conversion. It is the work of God's grace that gives us a new ability and understanding as the gospel is preached to us. In our own experience we become aware of our sin and need in the light of God's word, and appreciate the significance of the death of the Lord Jesus Christ when He died for our sin 'Being born again, not of corruptible seed, but of incorruptible, by the word of God, which liveth and abideth for ever' (1 Pet. 1:23). We can never be the same again, for now we belong to God. We are spiritually alive, with a new life before us. This life draws all its strength and comfort from God. 'Therefore if any man be in Christ, he is a new creature: old things are passed away; behold, all things are become new' (2 Cor. 5:17).

A new relationship

A miracle has happened. The wrath of God is turned away; the mercy of God is manifested in His Son. The sinner who, led by the Holy Spirit, has come in faith to the Saviour, is forgiven: 'In whom we have redemption through his blood, the forgiveness of sins, according to the riches of his grace' (Eph. 1:7). We can now approach our God and call Him our Father, because we come in the merits of His Son, the Lord Jesus Christ. The unworthy garment of our sinful life has been put on the Saviour, and the beautiful robe of His righteous life is placed on us. Thus we appear before God the Father in the merits of Jesus Christ. All this we acquire by faith. When our souls cry out for mercy, He grants us this faith, together with true sorrow and repentance for our sin: 'For by grace are ye saved through faith; and that not of yourselves: it is the gift of God' (Ephesians 2:8). When this miracle has taken place in us, we have peace with God, and inherit eternal life. We are assured that we shall never perish: 'My sheep hear my voice, and I know them, and they follow me: And I give unto them eterna life; and they shall never perish, neither shall any man pluck them out of my hand' (John 10: 27,28).

Now the fear of death and of judgment has been removed; because we have become the children of God. We rejoice in the physical resurrection of the Saviour, His conquest of death and of the grave. In our hearts is a glorious hope, for we know that death has lost its sting, and that one day we shall be like Him. One day He will give us a body like His own, and we shall worship and enjoy Him for ever. Sin no more shall trouble us, and we shall delight ourselves altogether in Him.

When I stand before the throne,
Dressed in beauty not my own;
When I see Thee as Thou art,
Love Thee with unsinning heart:
Then Lord, shall I fully know –
Not till then – how much I owe.

When we first come into this wonderful experience of knowing the Lord Jesus Christ, it is as if the whole world becomes new. We have been born again by the Holy Spirit; we have entered into a new life with a Saviour who is our Lord and Master. There is no greater joy in life than to know the Lord Jesus Christ as our own, and to know that from now on we belong to Him. His abiding presence will be with us, even unto the end of the world.

2. The Joy of Salvation

A source of deep comfort

The knowledge of our salvation is a source of deepest comfort to us. We belong to God Himself! This is a tremendous joy that can never be taken away from us: 'Who shall separate us from the love of Christ? Shall tribulation, or distress, or persecution, or famine, or nakedness, or peril, or sword? As it is written, For thy sake we are killed all the day long; we are accounted as sheep for the slaughter. Nay, in all these things we are more than conquerors through him that loved us. For I am persuaded, that neither death, nor life, nor angels, nor principalities, nor powers, nor things present, nor things to come, nor height, nor depth, nor any other creature, shall be able to separate us from the Love of God, which is in Christ Jesus our Lord' (Rom. 3:35-39). In times of deepest sorrow, when it seems as if all is against us, this knowledge will shine forth its comfort. For there are times – as in the life of King David when his family and friends rebelled against him – when all seems lost. As David, we shall find our strength in God: 'Why art thou cast down, O my soul? and why art thou disquieted within me? hope thou in God: for I shall yet praise Him, who is the health of my countenance, and my God' (Ps. 42:11). Never again shall we be utterly cast down, whatever our circumstances may be. Christians throughout the ages have suffered persecution, and have had to endure great tribulation and grief; yet their joy in the Lord has remained, because no power on earth was able to separate them from God. They often had to be separated from those who were dear to them; but from Him, never!

Our hearts are warmed when we think of those who are dear to us. We smile inwardly when we recall the happy ways of our children. We hurry homewards more quickly in joyful anticipation, with a glow in our hearts that words can never really express. If this is true on the human level, how much more is it true when we have been led to love the One who bled and died on the cross of Calvary, who rose victorious, and who is now seated at the right hand of God. How wonderful that by a miracle of grace He is with us both now and for ever! Our hearts cannot but rejoice in such a Saviour, such a Friend.

The ordinary becomes glorious

The daily life of any one of us, I suppose, can be most ordinary. Some days stand out with special significance, but most days pass by without any particular event to make them memorable. Yet, when we cherish this salvation in our hearts, there are no 'ordinary' days. Something has happened to our days. As each day unfolds, we meet it with a quiet confidence and courage. Our salvation is a kind of anchor which steadies us in the whirl of circumstances, and keeps us steadfast when we could easily drift. Life is richer now, because we are living to the glory and to the praise of God.

> Heaven above is softer blue,
> Earth around is sweeter green;
> Something lives in every hue,
> Christless eyes have never seen:
> Birds with gladder songs o'erflow,
> Flowers with deeper beauties shine,
> Since I know, as now I know
> I am His, and He is mine.

Our relationship with others

Our whole attitude has changed, and this is bound to affect our relationship with others. How easy it is for us to allow pride to creep into our lives at this point. Because we have been blessed with such a wonderful experience, and we see the spiritual barrenness of others who have no real knowledge of salvation, we can become proud in our attitude towards them. They will soon detect this and will resent it. There will always be the offence of the gospel; men will be offended and angry with us and our faith; but it is a different matter when our behaviour is the cause of the offence. Our attitude must be one of patience and love, with a desire that the other might be won for Christ. This does not mean that we should compromise, but it does mean that we must be gentle when we are firm, and that we must be understanding in our attitude.

We so soon forget what we were like, and the mercy that was shown to us. Sometimes we are prepared to stand for the cause of the gospel, but in a way which is far removed from the command of the Saviour. We are more ready to defend our cause than to stand as witnesses to His saving grace. We are to be bearers of good tidings, and we are to have a true concern for others. How can all this be? We are told of the constraining love of Christ, which will direct our thoughts and rule our behaviour. Men will know when we have been with Him. There will be a tenderness and a sympathy about us, which will have a touch of the compassion that we see in our Saviour. We must be approachable people, because we carry precious tidings.

Our inner light must shine

This salvation can glow not only in our hearts, but can also radiate in all our living, so that men and women will desire to know about the One who has made us new. Surely we should have the light of the hope of everlasting life in our eyes! In this dark world, where men live in the shadows of sin, let us shine as lights.

Let us remember who we are – we are the Lord's people. How often nations are judged by the few who happen to go abroad to distant lands. The impression they make by their behaviour is far-reaching, for their conduct will be regarded as typical of the country to which they belong. We too, as Christians, are constantly watched. Let us walk worthy of our Lord, so that we may be known for the faith we have toward God and the love that we show to one another. 'I therefore, the prisoner of the Lord, beseech you that ye walk worthy of the vocation wherewith ye are called' (Eph. 4:1).

6

THE RISEN LORD

The light and hope of the gospel had at last come to a world in darkness and weariness, where men hoped in vain and lived under the shadow of death. 'To give light to them that sit in darkness and in the shadow of death, to guide our feet into the way of peace' (Luke 1:79).

Something wonderful had happened. The ancient prophecies of the Word of God to the children of Israel had been fulfilled in the birth of Jesus Christ, the eternal Son of God. 'For unto us a child is born, unto us a son is given: and the government shall be upon his shoulder: and his name shall be called Wonderful, Counsellor, The mighty God, The everlasting Father, The Prince of Peace' (Isa. 9:6). Now in the fullness of time, foretold by the servants of the Lord, the long awaited Messiah, Jesus Christ, had been born. His birth was a miraculous one: He was born of a virgin. The place where He was born was a stable, because His parents failed to find accommodation in an inn. The simple manger cradled the Prince of Peace, the light of a world lay in the darkness of sin and death. It was this child who was to bring the hope of the gospel to the hearts and souls of men and women, bearing pardon for sin and the assurance of everlasting life.

1. The Author of Life

The Ability of the Person of Christ

The Bible clearly declares the divinity of Christ. We are presented with a Saviour who is able to save. 'God, who at sundry times and in divers manners, spake in time past unto the fathers by the prophets, Hath in these last days spoken unto us by his Son, whom he hath appointed heir of all things, by whom also he made the worlds' (Heb. 1:1,2). We praise God for the Lord Jesus Christ and His incarnation, for a Saviour who understands and is sympathetic to our frailty and poverty. In His human body He knew and experienced our limitations, yet graced humanity with such beauty.

Christ, by highest heaven adored,
Christ, the everlasting Lord,
Late in time behold Him come,
Offspring of a virgin's womb;
Veiled in flesh the Godhead see;
Hail the incarnate Deity!

Pleased as man with men to dwell,
Jesus, our Immanuel.

We praise God for His divinity, that in Him all the fullness of God dwells bodily. He is the only begotten Son of God, showing the same attributes, equal in majesty and power. 'Who, being in the form of God, thought it not robbery to be equal with God: but made himself of no reputation, and took upon him the form of a servant, and was made in the likeness of men' (Phil. 2:6,7). When we are confronted with the Lord in our salvation, it is with the eternal Son of God, who is the author and finisher of our faith. In Him there is power, life, grace and mercy towards us.

His life was one of obedience to the will of God. Our hearts are deeply moved as we learn the lessons He taught and read the accounts of His dealings with men and women. His life was full of grace and truth as He quietly yet resolutely set His face towards Jerusalem, and approached that final hour when He died on Calvary, paying the penalty for sin. But this was not the end.

The Reality of the Resurrection

When Mary sought the body of the Lord Jesus Christ at the tomb, she was confronted with an empty grave and the reality of a risen living

Saviour. At first she did not recognise Him, but did so as He called her by name. The Lord then instructed her to bear the tidings of His resurrection to His disciples. 'Touch me not; for I am not yet ascended to my Father: but go to my brethren and say unto them, I ascend unto my Father, and your Father; and to my God, and your God' (John 20:17).

The Lord also appeared to the disciples in the upper room although the doors were barred. On this occasion Thomas, one of the disciples, was missing and consequently was full of unbelief when told the news of the Saviour's resurrection, by the excited disciples. A week later, however, when Thomas was present, the Saviour appeared in their midst a second time. The Lord invited him to thrust both his finger into the wounds in His hands, and his hand into His pierced side. Thomas, convinced, said 'My Lord and my God' (John 20:28).

On another occasion two disciples were travelling to Emmaus sadly discussing the events of the past few days at Jerusalem. While they were engrossed in their conversation, the Lord Himself joined them. They did not recognise Him until they arrived at their journey's end. They invited Him to stay with them, and as He broke bread they recognised Him; then He vanished from their sight. Excitedly they referred to His conversation recalling how He opened the Scriptures and their hearts burned within them. They hastily returned to Jerusalem to tell the others.

Yet again at the sea of Tiberias the Lord was seen by the disciples. John recognised Him, but Peter jumped into the sea wading to the shore to go to Him. They were filled with wonder as they gazed upon Him while He dined with them. 'Jesus saith unto them, Come and dine, And none of the disciples durst ask Him, Who art Thou? knowing that it was the Lord' (John 21:12). For Peter, it was an unforgettable day, when the Saviour asked him three times 'Lovest thou me?' Peter full of remorse for his threefold denial at the time of the trial assured the Lord of his love and devotion. He was then commissioned to care for and feed the flock of God.

Its Special Significance

The resurrection of Jesus Christ has a special significance, which is distinct from any previous resurrection. If His resurrection were merely a re-uniting of body and soul and coming to life, He could not be described as 'the first fruits of them that slept'(1 Corinthians 15:20). The reason for this would be because we have recorded in the Gospels the raising of Lazarus, the daughter of Jairus and also the widow's son. What then made His resurrection so different? The risen body of the Lord Jesus Christ was physical and real, yet endowed with new qualities. We note His ability to appear behind closed doors, to vanish from sight, and to partake of food. Although He was not easily recognisable at first, the disciples knew that undeniably it was the Lord. We conclude that His risen body was without corruption, immortal but at the same time physical and tangible.

The resurrection appearances culminated in the final scene when the Lord ascended to heaven. He was seen by the disciples, 'And he led them out as far as to Bethany, and he lifted up his hands and blessed them. And it came to pass, while he blessed them, he was parted from them, and carried up into heaven. And they worshipped him, and returned to Jerusalem with great joy: And were continually in the temple, praising and blessing God' (Luke 24:50-53).

A Work of God

The truth of the resurrection sends a thrill of excitement through the gospel – He lives! It is an undeniable confirmation that the Lord Jesus Christ was all that He claimed to be. During His earthly ministry, the Lord spoke of His ability to lay down His life, and of His power to take it up again. More frequently, however, the references to the author of the resurrection point to the Father, 'Blessed be the God and Father of our Lord Jesus Christ, which according to His abundant mercy hath begotten us again unto a lively hope by the resurrection of Jesus Christ from the dead' (1 Pet. 1:3). The Holy Ghost also is included in this wonderful work, 'But if the Spirit of him that raised up Jesus from the dead dwell in you, he that raised up Christ from the dead shall also quicken your mortal bodies by his Spirit that dwelleth in you' (Rom. 8:11). There are many places that simply refer to God as the author of the resurrection. 'And God hath both raised up the Lord, and will also raise up us by his own power' (1 Cor. 6:14).

2. Partakers of Life

A truth that inspires

We worship a living Saviour who has conquered death, bringing a lively hope to the heart of the believer. Paul, in speaking of the resurrection, shows that our mortal and corruptible bodies cannot inherit the kingdom of God. 'For this corruptible must put on incorruption, and this mortal must put on immortality' (1 Cor. 15:53). Because of the truth of the risen Saviour, Paul is able to declare triumphantly 'O death, where is thy sting? O grave, where is thy victory?' (1 Cor. 15:55). For our faith is in a Saviour who has made this miracle possible for us. We too shall be clothed in immortality. We too shall be incorruptible. 'Therefore, my beloved brethren, be ye steadfast, unmoveable, always abounding in the work of the Lord, forasmuch as ye know that your labour is not in vain in the Lord' (1 Cor. 15:58).

Such a gospel and such a faith inspires the believer and fills him with joy and exultation. The resurrection proves that Jesus Christ was the long awaited Messiah, the Son of God, whose mission was redemption. The task He undertook involved Him in facing death in all its fullness for us, yet it was essential that it should end in life. This is a victorious, living Saviour, who died for us, but rose triumphant from the grave. The last enemy was dealt with, His work of redemption accomplished. Our future blessedness is assured because our Saviour lives.

The difference it makes

What difference does the teaching of the resurrection make to us? Can we ever be really the same when we are convinced of such a truth?

The hope we cherish in our hearts throbs with

life because we know that He conquered death. The dismal grave is not the end! How many have lived in fear of death, frightened by the very thought of its approach. Others choose to live as if there were no death, and fill their lives with ambition, work or pleasure. Some, however, made of sterner stuff, face it fearlessly with a determination that nothing shall ever cause them to tremble. Whatever our attitude the fact and reality of death remain. The Christian Gospel has something to say to us; that Jesus Christ has conquered death and we as believers shall live for ever with Him. Not only so, but one day we shall be fully equipped with our new immortal and incorruptible bodies.

When I tread the verge of Jordan,
Bid my anxious fears subside;
Death of death, and hell's destruction,
Land me safe on Canaan's side:
Songs of praises
I will ever give to Thee.

The assurance it gives

A new authority fills our hearts, as we witness and testify to His saving grace. By the Holy Spirit, He is literally with us, enabling us and supporting us. He is alive! Every part of our Christian life is filled with this truth, so that we cannot but rejoice. With deep reverence we come to the cross and His suffering, the grave and the mighty stone. We come even to the discarded cross, and an empty grave, but with joy in our hearts and expectant hope we come to a risen, ascended and glorified Saviour, the head of the Church.

Now we know that we are never alone, and substance is given to those promises that told us of His presence with us. There is no valley so dark, no desert so barren, no wilderness so wild in the experience of our lives that we need fear. For He is with us – even unto the end of the world. That even is not the end, for we shall see Him, we shall be like Him and we shall be with Him. 'Ye men of Galilee, why stand ye gazing up into heaven? This same Jesus which is taken up from you into heaven, shall so come in like manner as ye have seen him go into heaven' (Acts 1:11).

7

THE NARROW WAY

At one time or another most of us have admired the talents and abilities of others, and have longed that we too might display similar gifts. Alas! most of us seem to be born to a life of mediocrity. It does not always follow, however, that the gifted person makes the most marked contribution in life. On the contrary, more has often been achieved by the less able person, who plods along valiantly and uses to the full those abilities that he possesses. The reason for this is simply the ability of the latter to persevere.

1. Perseverance

Kept by the Power of God

The Biblical teaching of perseverance emphasises continuation of the work of grace begun in a believer by the Holy Spirit, until its completion in the sight of God. It is a great comfort to know that a work which God has begun will not be left unfinished. We were 'dead in trespasses and sins', and totally incapable of producing spiritual life within ourselves. It is God who implants spiritual life in us by the regenerating work of the Holy Spirit, and this issues in conversion through repentance and faith. If God has begun this work in us, we know that He has in view our ultimate salvation: 'Being confident of this very thing, that he which hath begun a good work in you will perform it until the day of Jesus Christ' (Phil. 1:6). We see, then that the true believer who has experienced the grace of God *will* persevere, *will* endure to the end. Perseverance begins, continues and ends with God, a point recognised by one writer who defines it as 'that continuous operation of the Holy Spirit in the believer, by which the work of divine grace that is begun in the heart is continued and brought to completion'. The Lord Jesus Christ said – 'My sheep hear my voice, and I know them, and they follow me: and I give unto them eternal life; and they shall never perish, neither shall any man pluck them out of my hand. My Father, which gave them me, is greater than all; and no man is able to pluck them out of my Father's hand' (John 10:27-29). Scripture is clear, however, about our activity, and steadfast pursuit of the things of God. He has provided for us adequate instructions which gives us a clear path to follow.

Perseverance – the very word itself is a rebuke to many of us. We have only to look at our bookshelves to find the sad evidence of things begun but never completed. How many courses have we begun at college or night school, and never finished? How many languages have we sought to learn? But now only a few forlorn books remain as a faded testimony to what might have been. This is the story of early enthusiasm, soon to be followed by indifference, and ending ultimately in complete forgetfulness. Most of us, if we are to make any real advance even in the most ordinary of pursuits, need both the stern discipline of a diligent teacher and the encouragement of friends.

Counting the Cost

But the condition of our souls, and our eternal destiny, can hardly be a matter of passing interest, to be abandoned indifferently on the bookshelf of past experiences. This is a matter of life and death! The salvation of our souls is a serious thing, deserving all our attention and the continuing application of mind and heart. We are well warned in Scripture not even to embark upon this way without having considered just what it will involve. We are told to count the cost, and we are shown the foolishness of an enthusiastic beginning, with no real desire for, or understanding of, the gospel of our Lord. Not only is it a superficial view of the truth; it is also a misleading one which deludes us into believing that we are the children of God when our hearts are still devoid of grace. We must consider well, and make sure that our faith is saving faith, and not an emotional or intellectual parody of it.

True faith involves mind, heart and will. We are warned by our Lord of the dangers of a hasty and thoughtless decision. In Luke's Gospel we read of the necessity of counting the cost, and of considering all that is involved in discipleship: 'If any man come to me, and hate not his father, and mother, and wife, and children, and brethren, and sisters, yea, and his own life also, he cannot be my disciple. And whosoever doth not bear his cross, and come after me, cannot be my disciple. For which of you, intending to build a tower, sitteth not down first, and counteth the cost, whether he have sufficient to finish it? Lest haply, after he hath laid the foundation, and is not able to finish it, all that behold it begin to mock him, saying, This man began to build, and was not able to finish' (Luke 14:26-30). This then is no hobby that we can take up and discard at our pleasure. Here we are involved with God, with the work of grace, and with everlasting life. It is not surprising that we are told 'he that endureth to the end shall be saved' (Matt. 10:22). If we know ourselves to be inconsistent and spasmodic in our interests, this condition of enduring to the end is alarming indeed! For, truly, if our ultimate salvation depended upon our endeavours to maintain a spiritual life in our own strength our prospects would be dismal in the extreme.

Response in our lives

The doctrine of perseverance is one of great comfort to us in the Christian life. We have learnt from experience in the bringing up of children how important it is to persevere with them, encouraging, rebuking, and guiding them – and always with their ultimate good in view. Sometimes we have almost despaired, and we would have given up, but for the fact that they were our own children and we loved them. By virtue of our perseverance they slowly respond, and eventually, so we trust, they will show in their lives the influence we have had upon them as parents. So God perseveres with us! It is comfort indeed to know that He will not let us go or give us up, but will persevere with His own.

This teaching has a very practical application for the believer who is confronted with a situation or a temptation that overwhelms him. How many times have we laboured and fought in our own strength, only to fail and to be bitterly disappointed with ourselves. It takes us a long time to realise our inability, and recognise the treachery of our own heart. When eventually we understand that if we trust in ourselves we are doomed to failure, then and only then will we seek the aid of the One who is able to help us in our need. When we find ourselves unable to overcome, unwilling to go on with the things of God, we see that we shall never endure to the end if we are left to ourselves. What a difference it makes then to realise that it is God who perseveres with us! If we cry to God to continue with us, in a most wonderful way we shall find ourselves persevering, resisting temptation, overcoming difficulties, because the Lord is in control. A new excitement comes to life, when we begin to look for the work of the Lord in our lives. We may sometimes wonder how He will wean us from some unworthy way and cause us to seek higher things. Yet when He works in us we shall stand amazed at His enabling grace in our lives.

Obedience

This does not mean, however, that we make no effort, leaving all to God. We are told in Scripture to strive, to fight, to run, to continue to the end. This we must do devoting all our mind and energy to this end. We know that it is God who works in us and sustains us, yet evidence of this is the resultant response in us. We must learn to heed the instructions of the work of God and abide by them. We must always endeavour to do His will with ready obedience and quick response, with steadfast and firm resolve to continue in the things of God and follow Him enduring to the end. The apostle Paul looking back on his Christian life was conscious of having fought a good fight of faith. It is the Christian's duty to keep the law of God. This means that we must learn to apply our energies to the performing of God's will. We are called upon to work out deliberately what our actions should be, in some situations, and our reactions in others. We have the instruction given in the Law of God, the Sermon on the Mount, and the Epistles, for our careful study and application. This calls for conscious effort. There will be times when this obedience is contrary to the natural desires of our hearts, but we must persevere. Yet at the same time we must always remember whence our strength comes, and that for all our very necessary determination, the enabling strength comes from God.

The secret of perseverance involves more than

a disciplined life and obedience to the will of God however, for there are times when it is extremely difficult to maintain the quiet composure of a heart at rest. As we are obedient, we become increasingly aware of the knowledge and presence of God in our lives. I would describe this experience as spiritual reality, when the glorious doctrines have become alive, and precious to our hearts and souls as well as to our minds. We honour the truths and exercise our minds fully in understanding the teachings of the Holy Scripture; yet we desire these very truths to lay hold of us that they may become real in our experience. Paul, writing to the Philippian Church says: 'I count all things but loss... That I may know him, and the power of his resurrection, and the fellowship of his sufferings, being made conformable unto his death' (Phil. 3:8,10). It is when we learn to desire the Saviour for His own sake that we begin to understand the meaning of true religion. Mere knowledge of the truth is thus transformed into fellowship with the Lord, and the truths about Him take on a new reality.

> My name from the palms of His hands
> Eternity will not erase;
> Impressed on His heart it remains
> In marks of indelible grace.

Yes, I to the end shall endure,
As sure as the earnest is given;
More happy, but not more secure,
The glorified spirits in heaven.

2. Sanctification

A new direction

Sanctification is that work of grace in the heart of a believer which affects the whole man: body, soul, intellect and affections. The Christian is called to follow God, to observe the law, and to devote his energies to the things of God. 'Knowing this that our old man is crucified with him, that the body of sin might be destroyed, that henceforth we should not serve sin' (Rom. 6:6). There must be evidence of a holy life and a deliberate turning away from sin. Something new has happened and is happening in the soul; the direction of the soul is changed and is daily strengthened in its God-ward path. It is not long before every part of the person is affected by this new directive. The whole nature is renewed and recognised by an active obedience in the performance of good works. Sanctification is a supernatural work of God in the life of the believer but He has provided means whereby the believer actively co-operates with the Holy Spirit in this work.

Holy Life

The work of *sanctification* in us, like that of perseverance, is primarily the work of God; but in both we are called upon to respond. In our sanctification we see the work of the Holy Spirit in operation, continuing and strengthening the aspirations after godliness now present in our hearts. As believers we should always be concerned for righteousness, because God Himself is righteous. When we consider our terrible unworthiness and sin in the sight of God, we can well believe the impossibility of salvation by our own works. We realise that we could never meet the requirements of the righteousness of God, which He reveals to us in His law. Yet the miracle happens; the unworthy is reckoned worthy in Christ. This is accompanied by a change of life, a desire to follow God and to live to His glory, His righteousness being imparted to us, and this confirms that we are the quickened and forgiven people of God. This is the work of grace in our lives.

What is our contribution as believers in this process of sanctification? The answer is clearly seen in the Word of God. We are told to walk in the light, to set our affections on the things that are above, and to love our brethren and our enemies. The Epistles were written to believers, and their constant appeal is for us to walk in the ways of God and to depart from our former sins. It is quite obvious that we are expected to obey the holy law of God, but with this significant difference, we are to do so in the strength of the Lord and not in our own. We must never forget at any time that 'it is God which worketh in you both to will and to do of his good pleasure' (Phil. 2:13). We are therefore faced with these two factors, firstly that it is the grace of God that works in us, and secondly, that we are called upon to be obedient to His will. We are fully aware that every holy desire springs from God, but when we find such desires lacking we will be alarmed and cry out to Him that He might stir us up to seek after Himself again. We cannot escape our personal responsibility for the state of our lives. We need constantly to make our calling and election sure.

The Implications in our lives

If we have known the mercy of God in the salvation of our souls, then we know full well that it is He alone who can produce in us the desire to seek after Him. Can our hearts ever forget the blessedness, the joy that was ours when first we knew Him as our Saviour? Once we are His, we can never be indifferent to Him. Even when we have sunk into apathy and sin, the approach of our God causes us to return again. It is the Lord who saved us, and He knows full well how to bring us back to Himself. Peter, his heart full of shame, wept bitterly in an agony of conscience-stricken memory, when the Lord turned and looked upon him. A believer can never forget his Lord. Each of our hearts is a throne, and it is His by right for He is our Lord as well as our Saviour. The sweetness of His presence makes obedience a delight and not merely a duty. We delight to do His good will because we love Him; like Peter, we too are able to say, 'Lord thou knowest all things; thou knowest that I love thee.' His presence, His words, His commands, and all that He is are precious to us. Godliness takes on a new meaning: it is to have the 'mind of Christ' formed in us (1 Cor. 2:16); it means 'bringing into captivity every thought to the obedience of Christ' (2 Cor. 10:5).

Constant attack

As Christians, whether we are aware of it or not, we are constantly exposed to attack. A godly life is a challenge to an ungodly world, which is held in the power of Satan and governed by the lusts of men. In every century the same pitiful story of hatred and pride, greed and cruelty is recorded.

Every now and again, nations and people have risen against the saints of God in merciless persecution. In less violent times, they single them out for contempt, misrepresentation, and mockery. The world has not changed. Our God has not changed either. But what about us?

> No wound? no scar?
> Yet, as the Master shall the servant be,
> And pierced are the feet that follow me;
> But thine are whole: can he have followed far
> Who has no wound nor scar?

As true believers, whatever the cost – and it will be costly – we must tread the narrow path of righteousness. At the same time, however, we shall experience many blessings along this path. We shall be led to still waters and green pastures at times, and our Lord will be with us in life and in death. As we are brought through such trials by His grace, we learn a little more about ourselves, and about the majesty of His person. We may bear the marks of battle, but we show also that we are the soldiers of Christ, the sons of God.

Are we willing travellers with Him on our pilgrimage? It has always been costly to tread such a pathway. We are called to be truthful where lies abound; to be pure when permissiveness encourages men to wallow in dreadful sin; to be silent when men abuse us; to be generous when offended. Who can lead such a life as this? No one on his own. But what is impossible with men becomes possible by the grace of God.

Take up thy cross, and follow Christ,
 Nor think till death to lay it down;
For only he who bears the cross
 May hope to wear the glorious crown.

There is no doubt as to the joy of such a life, because we are living for Christ Jesus. We become increasingly aware of His presence and God Himself becomes real to us. What we used to consider essential to our happiness in the affluent society of the twentieth century becomes small sacrifice indeed for us to give up at His request. There is no greater joy than fellowship with the Father and the Son by the Holy Spirit.

Such a life has purpose, and gives meaning to our existence. Our particular occupation may be drab and uninteresting. But now we have a new Master. He shines into the most mundane duty, and makes it a task worthwhile.

Inevitably there will be opposition, and oftentimes from the most unexpected quarters. But we must go on with Him. The godly path is a lonely one, and there are times when we stand alone and have to face much criticism and misunderstanding. Provided that this comes our way for the sake of the gospel, and not because we are seeking attention for ourselves, all is well. We must search our hearts and examine our motives. When we are sure we have discerned His will, however, we must act upon it, even though it may sometimes mean that we shall suffer for it, or be deprived of what we think we deserve. Even this is not without purpose, but is used for our good in the hands of God. He is ever directing and guiding us by our circumstances to greater godliness and deeper obedience. Let us use to the full every opportunity that He gives us.

We do not like to be unpopular, but at times we have to be for the sake of the gospel. We do not like to be lonely, and we shudder beneath the mockery of our associates. Yet even here there is a blessedness. 'Blessed are ye, when men shall revile you, and persecute you, and shall say all manner of evil against you falsely, for my sake. Rejoice and be exceeding glad: for great is your reward in heaven: for so persecuted they the prophets which were before you' (Matt. 5:11,12). In such an experience we may find that our Saviour becomes more dear, and more real to us, and new joys spring up in our hearts.

When once Thou visitest the heart,
Then truth begins to shine.

Christ never fails

How can we know Him in this way? Sometimes we find Him in the place of loneliness, as we endeavour to bear witness to the truth. Men shun us, but we find the promise true that He will never leave us nor forsake us. At other times it is in the valley of sorrow and distress, when perhaps weakness of body weighs heavily upon us. Although we suffer bodily illness as all men do, yet Satan would press us the harder with his cruel insinuations, crowding our hearts with doubts and fears. Yet again, it may be here that we find Him. At such times we know and prove the deep comfort of His presence. He uses affliction to teach us lessons more rapidly, and to apply them to our hearts. Through it we see more of the riches of His grace, and understand a little of His suffering and loneliness 'in the days of his flesh'. No one would seek to experience pain; and yet it is in the school of suffering that we often learn sweet lessons of the beautiful grace of our Saviour.

These and many other circumstances which befall us, are permitted in God's providence, so that we may seek Him. Slowly we learn that He is always there to succour and support us when we are tested and tried, to teach and to guide when we are perplexed and uncertain, to keep and guard us from all evil and despair. Before long we will learn to commune with Him for the sheer joy of doing so. We will learn to share all things with Him. We become more sensitive to the promptings of His Spirit, and learn what it is to pray without ceasing. The closer our walk with Him, the sweeter our lives will be.

The result of this close walk will begin to show in our lives, for we cannot live with a person without adopting many of his ways. The savour of Christ will be upon our lives, and obedience will no longer be a duty but a joy, because all we do is for Him and to please Him. To be in captivity to Him is freedom, because His presence is our joy. It is in this way that we grow in grace; but let us remember that it is by grace that we grow, and not by our own efforts. Knowledge is essential, the doctrines are precious; yet they are but servants to bring us to the Lord Jesus Christ. If we would grow in grace and endure to the end, then we must abide in the Author of grace.

Preservation

We will find that our fellowship with God will depend on how we continue in the ways of God. Satan will frequently attack us reminding us of our weaknesses and failures, which can bring despair to our hearts. Let us then remember that it is God who began a work in us and will complete that work. We must remember that God himself looks after our spiritual welfare. Nothing is wasted. In all situations He is guiding, teaching and bringing us to Himself. Our ultimate safety is assured. It is His intention to bring us safely to heaven one day where there is a place reserved for us. We are preserved even in this life so that one day we shall enjoy to the full the privileges of God's people. 'Now unto him that is able to keep you from falling, and to present you faultless before the presence of his glory with exceeding joy'(Jude 24).

8

THE WARFARE

Many of us will remember the rationing of essential food-stuffs and the shortage of luxury goods during World War Two. It became a familiar sight to see a shop full of people, and also queuing up outside, each one awaiting his turn. I can well remember the day when a consignment of apples had come in, and the local greengrocer's shop became resplendent with the welcome produce. I recall most clearly this particular event, because the lady in front of me in the queue boldly asked for an additional pound. The shop assistant looked up, amazement written all over her face and said 'Don't you know there's a war on, luv?'

I wonder if we as Christians are aware that there is a war on? How easy it is to accept the doctrines that relate to our salvation, and yet to bypass any reference to spiritual warfare. We can be amazingly ignorant of the wiles of the devil, and because of this we fall an easy prey to his attacks in times of stress. It is instructive to note how this spiritual battle is very clearly illustrated in the life of our Saviour: 'Then was Jesus led up of the Spirit into the wilderness to be tempted of the devil' (Matt. 4:1). Satan challenged Him by taunting Him as to His authority: 'If thou be the Son of God, command that these stones be made bread'. The Lord did not answer by performing some impressive act to convince Satan of His authority and divine Sonship, but in reply to each attack He quoted the Word of God. The Saviour's final reply to Satan at this encounter was: 'Get thee hence, Satan: for it is written, Thou shalt worship the Lord thy God, and him only shalt thou serve' (Matt. 4:10).

1. Spiritual Battle

The opposition of Satan

We are thus made aware of the spiritual battle that takes place. We may see Jesus Christ as Saviour and Lord, teacher, prophet, healer, a man of compassion, a brave and forthright person, and so He is. Yet the picture is incomplete, unless we also see Him opposing the powers of darkness arrayed in hatred against Him. We do not have to go far in the Gospels before we see Him casting out evil spirits and rebuking Satan.

The battle was the same for the apostles, as they were sent to bear the tidings of the gospel to many towns and cities. Nations that were once held in the grip of idolatry and darkness were now invaded by the light of the Word of God. We can well imagine the anger of Satan as these approached each town, and how he would oppose them both directly and indirectly, using every means at his disposal to cause dismay in their hearts and to destroy their work.

A clear example of this is when Paul was led by the Holy Spirit to Macedonia, to the city of Philippi. It was not long before the powers of evil manifested themselves in a servant girl: 'And it came to pass, as we went to prayer, a certain damsel possessed with a spirit of divination met us, which brought her masters much gain by soothsaying: The same followed Paul and us, and cried, saying, These men are the servants of the most high God, which shew unto us the way of salvation' (Acts 16:16,17). Paul recognised the evil spirit in this girl, and 'being grieved, turned and said to the spirit, I command thee in the name of Jesus Christ to come out of her. And he came out the same hour' (Acts 16:18). It is then that we see the anger of Satan unleashed against these men of God, using this situation to rouse the violence of the city against them: 'And when her masters saw that the hope of their gains was gone, they caught Paul and Silas, and drew them into the marketplace unto the rulers' (Acts 16:19).

Things looked black indeed, and there followed flogging, disgrace, imprisonment and humiliation.

On active service

How slow we are to understand that we are still at war, and that Satan will do all in his power to hinder the Lord's work and to harm the saints. We know that he is not able to sever us from our Saviour, that once we are redeemed there is no power on earth or in hell that is able to separate us from our God. But Scripture tells us how Satan, 'as a roaring lion, walketh about seeking whom he may devour' and how at other times he may appear as 'an angel of light', deceiving even if it were possible, the very elect of God. 'For there shall arise false Christs, and false prophets, and shall shew great signs and wonders; insomuch that, if it were possible, they shall deceive the very elect' (Matt. 24:24). In the Epistle to the Ephesians, Paul tells us of this spiritual battle: 'For we wrestle not against flesh and blood, but against principalities, against powers, against the rulers of the darkness of this world, against spiritual wickedness in high places' (Eph. 6:12).

It is sad, but true, that despite the warnings and advice of Scripture, we are ill equipped for such a savage battle and such a brutal foe. So great is our indifference and our vanity that we believe that somehow we will be able to cope on our own. Some believe that they are invulnerable to attacks by the very fact that they are Christians. Such are like soldiers without equipment, roaming aimlessly in no man's land, resting on the assurance that they belong to the British Army. This is a serious battle, and the issues have greater and more lasting consequences than any earthly battle, for eternal life and death are at stake.

The Enemy and his Limitations

Let us consider the enemy, whose tactics are described in Scripture as the 'wiles of the devil'. We are left in no doubt in the Bible as to the personality of Satan. But how great is his power and what are his limitations? In any battle it is important to know the strength of the enemy and something about his methods of attack. How does Satan compare with God in power and ability?

Satan is *not omnipotent*, but is mighty. Nevertheless let us remember that wc cannot hope to match him in our own strength. It is instructive to notice how 'Michael the archangel, when contending with the devil he disputed about the about body of Moses, durst not bring against him a railing accusation, but said, The Lord rebuke thee'(Jude 9). We see here that an archangel cannot on his own rebuke Satan. This is a solemn reminder to us of Satan's authority and power, which is far in excess of our own.

Satan is *not omniscient*, but he is well informed. He does not know what goes on in our hearts. He can come to the 'frontiers of the mind', and present his evil schemes; but it is God alone who knows the heart of man. Satan and his agents are sufficiently well informed, by observing our most vulnerable parts and weaknesses, to exploit them to his best advantage. We can recognise something of his strategy in this sphere as Satan nags and drives the sinner relentlessly.

Satan is *not omnipresent,* but is limited by only being able to be at one place at a time. For all that, we must not deceive ourselves into thinking that our turn to be tempted by him will seldom come round. He works through a host of evil spirits or fallen angels. These are disembodied spirits who wander at his will, know his evil mind and purpose, and faithfully serve their dreadful master. Their end is doom, but with Satan they scheme all manner of wickedness to keep men in darkness, to harass the Church, and to bring confusion and destruction to believers.

Satan is *not immutable*, but changes with regard to his moods and schemes. Living on lies, in ever changing approaches he constantly presents new fronts to us. 'He was a murderer from the beginning, and abode not in the truth, because there is no truth in him. When he speaketh a lie, he speaketh of his own: for he is a liar, and the father of it' (John 8:44). We learn of the unfaithfulness and deception of Satan.

A subtle foe

We see then that our adversary is mighty, but not almighty, well informed but not omniscient. Although served by a host of spirits, neither he nor they are omnipresent. And finally, he is a foe of changing faces and moods, deeply deceptive, a liar. This is Satan, the enemy of God and of His people.

It is important for us to clarify what we mean by 'temptation'. We are often tempted by the lust of our own hearts, and in our very frailty we would easily give way to it 'every man is tempted, when he is drawn away of his own lust, and enticed' (Jas. 1:14). The word 'temptation' is also used in Scripture in the sense of being tried or tested of the Lord for his own eternal purposes in our souls: 'That the trial of you faith, being much more precious than of gold that perisheth, though it be tried with fire, might be found unto praise and honour and glory at the appearing of Jesus Christ' (1 Pet. 1:7). With a very different end in view, Satan can come upon us to tempt us for evil purposes. Satan tempts oftentimes using to his advantage the sin of our own heart as well to further his wicked plans.

2. Our Commitment in His War

Our Equipment

How shall we fare in battle against such a foe? It is obvious that we cannot stand on our own, and must learn to draw on the vast resources of God. We are instructed to stand, to stand in the face of attacks from Satan. But how can we do this? We are given excellent instructions in the Bible as to how we should enter into the battle, and how we should be equipped. Although we must be fully aware of the wiles of Satan, our preoccupation must be with our equipment and resources. 'Wherefore take unto you the whole armour of God, that ye may be able to withstand in the evil day, and having done all, to stand' (Eph. 6:13).

In his description of the soldier's equipment for this spiritual battle Paul is careful of detail. He tells us to 'Stand therefore, having your loins girt about with truth' (Eph. 6:14). We thus begin with the truth of the gospel of our God: 'In whom ye also trusted, after that ye heard the word of truth, the gospel of your salvation' (Eph. 1:13). We must be right here, we must know and believe the fundamental truths of the glorious gospel, of the divine Redeemer who came to save us.

Paul then bids us to wear 'the breastplate of righteousness' (Eph. 6:14). As truth is basic, girding the loins, so righteousness is vital, covering our vulnerable heart. This righteousness is the merit of the Lord Jesus Christ, for not only did He pay the penalty for sin and unrighteousness, but also His sinless life is counted to the sinner's credit.

Thus in facing the foe, we are to be equipped consciously relying upon truth, radiating truthfulness in all our being; we are to be covered with the righteousness of Christ, so that we leave no place for a fierce accuser to find fault with us. We must be aware that the Lord Jesus Christ is the living truth. We know him by believing and declaring the truth of the Word of God. Satan the father of lies will tremble at the very name of Him who is this Truth.

Roman soldiers were well shod: this enabled them to march long distances, and take the enemy by surprise, and it assured the Roman Empire of victory after victory. 'And your feet shod with the preparation of the gospel of peace' (Eph. 6:15). The gospel brings peace to the hearts of men and women, and we are to be bearers of the tidings which will liberate those who are held in darkness and the slavery of sin. Peace has now been made;

the Lord Jesus Christ has died for our sins, and we have peace with God. Let us be untiring in our efforts to proclaim this: 'How beautiful are the feet of them that preach the gospel of peace, and bring glad tidings of good things' (Rom. 10:15).

An essential part of the soldier's equipment was the shield, which was designed to be manoeuvred quickly, to protect exposed parts of the body. The enemy often shot flaming arrows, and the soldier would dip his shield in water before the battle so that these would be extinguished. The Christian is to take 'the shield of faith, wherewith ye shall be able to quench all the fiery darts of the wicked' (Eph. 6:16). This faith includes the saving faith which is a gift from God. It is no personal effort of our own, whereby we offer our frail trust to the Lord Jesus Christ, for that is as unreliable as we ourselves. It is the faith that He grants to the sinner who calls upon Him for mercy – 'For by grace are ye saved through faith; and that not of yourselves: it is the gift of God' (Eph. 2:8). Not only are we saved by faith in Christ, but we become men and women who live by faith. Whatever fiery dart Satan may hurl, let us hold up the shield, tell him that we believe the gospel, and that we are the Lord's.

Another part of the Christian's armour is 'the Helmet of Salvation'. There is a great battle for the minds of men and women in our day. We are bombarded by all manner of credible but miserable things, such as humanism, atheism, modernism, Roman Catholicism and the various cults. Yet it is not new. Satan has used this device down through the centuries, but God has provided us with the helmet of salvation. We must learn to have the mind of Christ. How easy it is for us to play with sin at first, and soon to wander far into it, imperceptibly, almost unnoticed. Yet Satan has gained a foothold. We ought constantly to remind ourselves that 'though we walk in the flesh, we do not war after the flesh: (For the weapons of our warfare are not carnal, but mighty through God to the pulling down of strongholds;) Casting down imaginations, and every high thing that exalteth itself against the knowledge of God, and bringing into captivity every thought to the obedience of Christ' (2 Cor. 10: 3-5). We must learn to confess such thoughts to the Saviour and seek His deliverance from them. We must garrison our minds with the truths of the gospel, and be well instructed in the principles of Scripture. We must 'take the helmet of salvation' (Eph. 6:17).

The Word of God is the sword of the Spirit. When the Saviour was tempted in the wilderness, He answered Satan with this Word. We also need to learn the value of the Word, which is 'sharper than any two-edged sword' (Heb. 4:12). 'Take... the sword of the Spirit, which is the word of God' (Eph. 6:17). We must learn it, know it and use it in the battle.

Use your resources

We are told to put on this armour consciously that we may be able to stand against the wiles of the devil. Our advance must be prayerful. We must keep close to our God. Oftentimes dark shadows and depression come upon us for no apparent reason, and our souls groan within us. There are times when Satan sends, as it were, a draught from hell upon us, and something of its dismal horror chills our souls. We must be alert, aware of his tactics, learning to draw swiftly on the resources of God. We must be able to recognise evil when we see it, to know that we cannot cope unaided or ill-equipped, and to don the armour of God. If Satan can bring despair to our hearts he has gained a victory, and this we must never allow. He is full of insinuations about other people, attractive temptations, and a host of similar devices, and is waiting to pour them into our frail hearts: But 'be strong in the Lord, and in the power of his might' (Eph. 6:10).

An unrelenting conflict

We are in this battle every day. I do not mean that we should allow ourselves to become so engrossed and preoccupied with the powers of evil that we see no good in anything, suspect every motive, and attribute everything to the work of Satan. We must learn to be discerning. Satan can sometimes use us when we rashly take decisions without consulting the Lord. We must also see that the battle is not against individuals, however difficult they may be at times. Our battle is against the Enemy himself, and not against the people he is using. When we realise this, we are thrown more and more upon the Lord, and we learn more of the power of prayer. We will begin to assess things correctly, and to understand what needs to be done in the different situations that confront us.

When we realise fully that 'we wrestle not against flesh and blood' but against the powers of evil, we shall be less tempted to strive 'in the flesh'. We will see that we have to learn how to draw on the vast resources of our God. The name of Jesus will become exceedingly precious to us, the name that spells fear in the heart of Satan and his evil servants.

From Scripture we have learnt something of the extent and limitations of Satan's power and activity. It is a great comfort to know that Satan's might is more than matched with the almighty power of God. We realise that Satan's knowledge is extensive but he has not the omniscience of God, who knows our hearts. We believe in and know of God's omnipresence. Satan, however, limited to one place at a time, must depend on his evil servants to harass and deceive mankind. We must not underestimate our foe, but we can be comforted in the knowledge of our great and incomparable God. This God in His mercy has come to our aid 'For this purpose the Son of God was manifested, that he might destroy the works of the devil' (1 John 3:8).

9

THE PROMISE

How many times have we heard Christians complain of their inability to witness effectively to the Gospel of the Lord Jesus Christ, explaining how this has saddened and frustrated them in their Christian life. This cry of ineffectiveness and inability has been echoed by many preachers, as they long for power in their preaching, and for ministries which are more effective. Men have searched their hearts, and in an attempt to remedy this defect have intensified their efforts in visitation and endless activities.

As we read the Acts of the Apostles, a very different picture is presented to us. Here we meet a handful of men who are turning the world upside down. They travelled much, they preached, they suffered, and they were successful. What was their secret? We must admit that there is a great difference between their witness and ours. Yet should it be so? Is it likely that the power granted to them should be withheld from later generations? The task begun then – going out into the whole world to preach the gospel – remains the same today. There is no mention in the Scriptures that the enabling gifts granted then were to be taken away, nor any suggestion that they had been intended exclusively for the apostolic age.

A deficiency remedied

The apostle Paul, whilst on one of his journeys, came to Ephesus, and found there certain disciples. When he met them, he was immediately aware that there was something radically wrong with them. It is often debated whether they were actually Christians. What is important for us to notice, however, is that Paul regarded them as Christians. We can be sure of this for two reasons. In the first place they are referred to as disciples, and in the New Testament the term disciples, unless qualified by connection with a specifically named person, always refers to those who are disciples of the Lord Jesus Christ. Secondly, Paul's remark to them, 'Have ye received the Holy Ghost since ye believed?' (Acts 19:2), would hardly have been addressed to unbelievers. We gather, therefore, that in Paul's reckoning it is possible to be a believer, and still not to have 'received the Holy Ghost'. Yet we know Paul believed that a man cannot be a Christian without the regenerating work of the Holy Spirit, and that the Spirit indwells and sanctifies all whom He has regenerated. 'Now if any man have not the Spirit of Christ, he is none of his' (Rom. 8:9). Paul, however, is asking them here if they have received the Holy Spirit *since* they believed. It is clear that they have no knowledge of Him, nor do they know the experience of which Paul speaks. We are told that they were then baptised in the name of the Lord Jesus: 'And when Paul had laid his hands upon them, the Holy Ghost came on them; and they spake with tongues, and prophesied' (Acts 19:6).

A remembered experience

In his letter to the Ephesians, Paul reminds the church again of this experience: 'In whom ye also trusted, after that ye heard the word of truth, the gospel of your salvation: in whom also after that ye believed, ye were sealed with that holy Spirit of promise' (Eph. 1:13). To the Ephesians at that time, and also to us today, the phrase 'sealed with that holy Spirit of promise' is surely significant. What is the promise to which it refers? We find the answer in Acts 2:16-21: 'this is that which was spoken by the prophet Joel; And it shall come to pass in the last days, saith God, I will pour out of my Spirit upon all flesh: and your sons and your daughters shall prophesy, and your young men shall see visions, and your old men shall dream dreams: And on my servants and on my handmaidens I will pour out in those days of my Spirit: And they shall prophesy: and I will show wonders in heaven above and signs in the earth beneath'. From this we understand that the promise was to be fulfilled in 'the last days' – that period of time extending from the first coming of our Lord to His second coming. We ourselves are therefore living in this period. But where do we find this promise fulfilled and manifested in our witness and ministry? For whom is it intended? We realise that there is a sense in which Pentecost is unique and cannot be repeated, for this tremendous outpouring of the Holy Spirit upon the newly formed church was to establish her, and to give her power and authority. Yet there is a sense too in which the promise is intended for believers in all ages. We too are included within its scope. We cannot repeat Pentecost; but by the grace of God we can still receive the same unction of the Spirit, to make our witnessing and preaching effective in this age. Let us look again at the way Peter, in addressing the multitude, referred to the promise: 'Then Peter said unto them, Repent, and be baptised every one of you in the name of Jesus Christ for the remission of sins, and ye shall receive the gift of the Holy Ghost. For the promise is unto you, and to your children, and to all that are afar off, even as many as the Lord our God shall call' (Acts 2:38,39). We might conclude that this promise was for the apostolic age only, but for two points. Firstly we could hardly believe that he reference to the remission of sins was intended only for first century man. Secondly, that last phrase 'as many as the Lord our God shall call' surely includes us. The promise is for us also.

A gift of Christ

All this is leading us to an experience, a 'baptism', that the early church knew well. 'For John truly baptised with water; but ye shall be baptised with the Holy Ghost not many days hence' (Acts 1:5). It is quite clear what was the purpose of this baptism. 'But ye shall receive power, after that the Holy Ghost is come upon you: and ye shall be witnesses unto me both in Jerusalem, and in all Judaea, and in Samaria, and unto the uttermost part of the earth' (Acts 1:8). When we consider the life and ministry of the Lord Jesus Christ, we learn that He fulfilled His earthly ministry by the power of the Holy Spirit. We find a number of references to this in Luke's Gospel: 'Now when all the people were baptised, it came to pass, that Jesus also being baptised, and praying, the heaven was opened, And the Holy Ghost descended in a bodily shape like a dove upon him, and a voice came from heaven, which said, Thou art my beloved Son; in thee I am well pleased' (Luke 3:21,22); 'Jesus being full of the Holy Ghost returned from Jordan, and was led by the Spirit into the wilderness' (Luke 4:1); 'Jesus returned in the power of the Spirit into Galilee: and there went out a fame of him through all the region round about' (Luke 4:14); 'The Spirit of the Lord is upon me, because he hath anointed me to preach the gospel to the poor; he hath sent me to heal the brokenhearted, to preach deliverance to the captives, and recovering of sight to the blind, to set a liberty them that are bruised' (Luke 4:18). When the ministry of our Saviour is referred to in the book of Acts, the fact is duly recognised that His earthly ministry was fulfilled in the power of the Holy Spirit: 'God anointed Jesus of Nazareth with the Holy Ghost and with power: who went about going good, and healing all that were oppressed of the devil; for God was with him' (Acts 10:38).

We know that it was necessary also for the disciples to receive this baptism, which would enable them to do mighty works. Is it possible that we should believe that we can continue in the flesh what was begun in the power of the Holy Spirit?

A distinct experience

It is obvious that the baptism with the Holy Spirit is a distinct and personal experience, not to be confused with regeneration or with sanctification. The Christian who has not received this baptism must not be regarded as in any way inferior; for this would be to belittle the work of the Holy Spirit in regeneration. In a sense the baptism of the Spirit is a direct work upon the believer, intensifying his knowledge of God and granting power in testimony. John Flavel, in relating the experience of a minister, generally taken to be himself, says:

'In all the day's journey he neither met, overtook, nor was overtaken by any. Thus going on his way his thoughts began to swell, and rise higher and higher like the waters in Ezekiel's vision, till at last they became an overwhelming flood. Such was the intention of his mind, such the ravishing tastes of heavenly joys, and such the full assurance of his interest therein, that he utterly lost sight and sense of this world and all the concerns thereof: and for some hours he knew no more where he was than if he had been in a deep sleep upon his bed... after a few hours he was sensible of the ebbing of the tide, and before night, though there was the heavenly serenity and sweet peace upon his spirit which continued long with him, yet this transport of joy was over and the fine edge of his delight blunted. He many years after called that day one of the days of heaven and professed he understood more of the life of heaven by it than by all the books he ever read or discourses he ever entertained about it'.

There is an interval of time, short as it may be in some cases, between conversion and receiving the baptism of the Spirit. The primary purpose of this baptism is that we might know God more deeply, and that our witness might be powerful, so that we might speak in the Spirit rather than in our own strength. 'But ye shall receive power, after that the Holy Ghost is come upon you: and ye shall be witnesses unto me both in Jerusalem, and in all Judæa, and in Samaria, and unto the uttermost part of the earth' (Acts 1:8). In Luke we read that the disciples are told that they are to be witnesses to the truth: Jesus 'said unto them, Thus it is written, and thus it behoved Christ to suffer, and to rise from the dead the third day: And that repentance and remission of sins should be preached in his name among all nations, beginning at Jerusalem. And ye are witnesses of these things' (Luke 24:46-48).

But how were they to achieve this? They were told of the promise which should be theirs: 'Behold, I send the promise of my Father upon you: but tarry ye in the city of Jerusalem, until ye be endued with power from on high' (Luke 24:49). When Peter stood before the Sanhedrin, he witnessed bravely to that court: 'The God of our fathers raised up Jesus, whom ye slew and hanged on a tree. Him hath God exalted with his right hand to be a Prince and a Saviour, for to give repentance to Israel, and forgiveness of sins. And we are his witnesses of these things; and so is also the Holy Ghost, whom God hath given to them that obey him' (Acts 5:30-32). As we read the account of their labours, we become increasingly conscious that these men were full of the Holy Ghost, and that their work and ministry was carried out in His power.

Its effect

The effect of the baptism with the Holy Spirit was very pronounced in the life of the disciples. There is a deep sense of the glory and of the presence of God in their lives, a fear and awe also of God. There is too, a keener sense of joy and gladness. We see them rejoicing even in tribulation. Paul and Silas, after being flogged and then chained in the inner prison, sing praises to God. The love of God floods their hearts, as in the case of Stephen, forgiving his murderers as he is brutally stoned to death. What makes men behave like this, if it is not an unction from on high? We see men fervently witnessing, preaching boldly the unsearchable riches of Christ, daunted by nothing as they journey forth on their divine errand. Again, simple fishermen, such as Peter and John, write with a profound understanding of the deep things of God. These men are changed. 'But ye have an unction from the Holy One, and ye know all things' (1 John 2:20).

Can we know it?

How shall *we* receive such a gift, that we too might see the mighty works of God in our own day? We are weary of the fleeting value of work done in our own strength, and long to see a true work of God.

There is an account in the Gospel of Luke of how a man sought assistance of his friend, because a visitor had called on him and he had no bread for him. The friend was in bed. Eventually however, he complied with his persistent demands, and gave him sufficient bread for his visitor. 'If a son shall ask bread of any of you that is a father, will he give him a stone? or if he ask a fish, will he for a fish give him a serpent? or if he shall ask an egg, will he offer him a scorpion? If ye then, being evil, know how to give good gifts unto your children: how much more shall your heavenly Father give the Holy Spirit to them that ask him?' (Luke 11:11-13).

Is it not true that, though we have fed on the bread of life, and salvation is ours, yet when strangers come by, we have no bread to offer? When we receive the Holy Spirit, there comes a new ability whereby sinners can be fed with the bread of life. We need to seek this baptism, this unction, so that many may be blessed through us. We are told simply to ask, but with true, heartfelt desire. We cannot ask lightly, or with an unbelieving heart. Although it would be wrong to lay down conditions, we can say that our asking must be earnest and sincere. If this is so, there will be a thirsting and a longing for the things of God, and an attentiveness to godliness in our lives. On the other hand, we can hardly be in earnest if we are asking with deliberate sin and disobedience in our hearts. Satan will readily provide a counterfeit for the carnal Christian who refuses to leave his undisciplined life, and who merely seeks the blessing for its own sake, delighting in the thrill of an experience, but shunning the weightier matters of the law and of involvement with God. Let us ask believing, desiring His glory, and obeying His Word. 'And I say unto you, Ask, and it shall be given you; seek, and ye shall find; knock, and it shall be opened unto you. For every one that asketh receiveth; and he that seeketh findeth; and to him that knocketh it shall be opened' (Luke 11:9,10).

The baptism with the Holy Spirit is not to be confused with, or in any way equated with, what the Bible has to say concerning our sanctification. Moreover, a clear distinction must be drawn between the experience and any kind of perfectionist teaching. Yet nevertheless it has a great and profound effect upon our lives. We enter a new spiritual dimension. We are given a true realisation of our own inadequacy and at the same time a simple trust in the absolute and sovereign ability of God. When we realise that any lasting work is of the Lord, and we see that we are not indispensable, false humility has lost its place. This makes us spiritually realistic. In our hearts we recognise Him and honour Him. Such knowledge keeps us humble. We know that He could take His Spirit from us, and leave us helpless and forlorn, struggling again in our own strength.

In our witnessing a real change has taken place. When we are taking a meeting we prepare in the same way as before; but He is with us in greater power. Our simple efforts, faithful as they must be to the truth, are applied more effectively by the Holy Spirit to the hearts of men and women. New opportunities are given by the Lord. We are kept fully occupied, but gone is the frenzied activity of self in its anxiety to do the work of God. This calls for an obedient heart, a quiet walk, a sensitivity to the promptings of the Holy Spirit.

It is then that the seed of revival is born in our hearts. Not revival in the sense of a mighty awakening which stirs up the slumbering church, and which sweeps men into the kingdom, but that quality of spirituality on a personal level which is so evident in times of revival, albeit on a larger scale. While we wait for revival in this sense, let us seek the things of the Spirit and be occupied in the affairs of His kingdom. 'For from you sounded out the word of the Lord not only in Macedonia and Achaia, but also in every place your faith to God-ward is spread abroad; so that we need not to speak any thing' (1 Thess. 1:8).

Spirit of God, descend upon my heart;
Wean it from earth; through all its pulses move;
Stoop to my weakness, mighty as Thou art,
And make me love Thee as I ought to love.

Teach me to love Thee as Thine angels love,
One holy passion filling all my frame –
The baptism of the heaven-descended Dove,
My heart an altar, and Thy love the flame.

10

THE CONSUMMATION

I can remember, when we were children at home, how we looked forward to friends who visited us. Amongst these welcome guests was the minister of our little chapel, of whom we were particularly fond. When the time came for him to leave, we would always ask eagerly, 'When are you coming again?' The visit of a loved one is looked forward to with joy and anticipation.

The first coming of the Lord Jesus Christ was foretold by prophets and heralded by John the Baptist. At last the day dawned when Jesus Christ was born in a humble stable at Bethlehem in Judea. As was His birth, so was His life, simple and pure, acceptable in the sight of God and men. He preached the message of the kingdom of God, healed the sick, opposed the powers of evil, and finally died on the cross to pay the penalty for our sin. The grave could not hold Him, the author of life, and in three days God raised Him from the dead. Before He finally ascended to heaven, He appeared to the disciples on a number of occasions over a period of forty days. The time came when He gathered His disciples together and gave them the commission to preach the gospel, promising that before long He would send the Holy Spirit to them, so that they would be endued with power from on high. 'And he led them out as far as to Bethany, and he lifted up his hands, and blessed them. And it came to pass, while he blessed them, he was parted from them, and carried up into heaven' (Luke 24:50,51). The disciples gazed upon the departure of their Lord, unaware that standing beside them were two angels: 'And while they looked steadfastly toward heaven as he went up, behold, two men stood by them in white apparel; Which also said, Ye men of Galilee, why stand ye gazing up into heaven? this same Jesus, which is taken up from you into heaven, shall so come in like manner as ye have seen him go into heaven' (Acts 1:10,11).

1. The Return of the Lord

He will come again

The promise that the Lord Jesus Christ will come a second time is referred to over three hundred times in the Scriptures. From these references a great deal of speculation has arisen during the long history of the Christian Church as to the time of the Lord's coming. Although we are given signs to look for which will precede the coming of the Lord Jesus Christ, it is wrong to seek to determine the exact date. 'But of that day and hour knoweth no man, no, not the angels of heaven, but my Father only' (Matt. 24:36). It is certain that the time draws nigh, but we dare not speculate, even though we must always be ready for His return. In the early Church the Christians at Thessalonica allowed their eager expectancy of this event to dominate their lives, so that their work and ordinary occupations suffered. Paul, in writing to them, gently rebukes them, whilst furnishing them with further detail: 'Let no man deceive you by any means: for that day shall not come, except there come a falling away first, and that man of sin be revealed, the son of perdition' (2 Thess. 2:3).

Personally

It is quite clearly stated in Scripture, that the coming of the Lord will be *personal* – 'this same Jesus . . . in like manner'. There have been many vague half-truths propounded, such as that the Lord's coming is when He comes for us at death. This in no way does justice to the clear and definite teaching of Scripture regarding His personal return. 'Therefore be ye also ready: for in such an hour as ye think not the Son of man cometh' (Matt. 24:44).

Visibly

The reality of His physical return as a future event is shown to us, and it will be unmistakable. 'Behold, he cometh with clouds; and every eye shall see him, and they also which pierced him: and all kindreds of the earth shall wail because of him. Even so, Amen' (Rev. 1:7). The coming of our Saviour will be a visible coming.

Gloriously

We shall see Him, and for His people the sight will be a glorious one. The Church of Jesus Christ is likened unto a bride awaiting the coming of the bridegroom. The event will be one of great splendour and glory, striking fear into the hearts of unbelievers, but joy into the hearts of those who have long expected Him. 'And then shall appear the sign of the Son of man in heaven: and then shall all the tribes of the earth mourn, and they shall see the Son of man coming in the clouds of heaven with power and great glory. And he shall send his angels with a great sound of a trumpet, and they shall gather together his elect from the four winds, from one end of heaven to the other' (Matt. 24:30,31).

Suddenly

There will be an element of the unexpected in His coming. Despite the fact of signs and events pointing and leading to His second coming, it will arrive like a thief in the night. Men will be busy in the affairs of this life, and the time will arrive when they least expect it, despite the many warnings – 'Watch, therefore: for ye know not what hour your Lord doth come' (Matt. 24:42). When He comes this second time it will be with splendour and authority. He will be in royal apparel, and will be heralded by angels and a mighty shout. It will be a triumphal entry, the culmination of all things, for we learn that His coming again and the end of the world are at the same time.

To Judgment

We shall witness the resurrection of the dead. Those who have died in Christ He will bring with Him, and those who are alive at His coming shall be caught up to meet their Saviour in the air. Nor is the physical resurrection confined to Christians, but the bodies of unbelievers are also reunited with their souls. The mighty judgment shall then be heralded and God shall judge all mankind. 'And I saw the dead, small and great, stand before God; and the books were opened:

and another book was opened, which is the book of life: and the dead were judged out of those things which were written in the books, according to their works. And the sea gave up the dead which were in it; and death and hell delivered up the dead which were in them: and they were judged every man according to their works. And death and hell were cast into the lake of fire. This is the second death. And whosoever was not found written in the book of life was cast into the lake of fire' (Rev. 20:12-15). These events foretold in Scripture move us to a deep reverence, in the knowledge that our Saviour will come to His Church in the midst of her trial and affliction, and will triumphantly gather His people to Himself. We are conscious too that in that great day God will judge great and small in perfect righteousness. There will be no persuasiveness that will be able to deceive Him, for He will know us for what we are. The redeemed will be known by the grace that has been granted to them, the lost will be known by their rebellion. The finality of such a judgment brings a soberness to our hearts, so that our faith cannot be taken lightly. Though there is a spirit of eager expectancy as to His glorious return, yet we know that this is associated with the day of judgment.

2. The Expectation of His Return

Watch ye therefore

The fact of this in itself causes us concern, that our lives might be obedient to His will. We cannot afford to be wasteful of our time or flippant in our attitude. We must seek, by the grace of God, to pluck men as 'brands from the burning'. Our lives should be an example to those around us, showing that we live expecting our Saviour. We do this by redeeming the time and occupying ourselves with the things of God. We live our lives knowing that we have to give an account to God. All men shall appear before Him, and as believers we also shall appear before His Judgment throne. Will He say to us on that day, 'Well done, thou good and faithful servant' (Matt. 25:21)? Or will He say 'I never knew you: depart from me, ye that work iniquity' (Matt. 7:23)?

Preparedness

We have all known from experience how easy it is to neglect our studies, to act as if there were no examination. Then suddenly, as the day approaches, we intensify our preparations. But the date of examination is known, whereas the date of His return is not known, but we do need to be prepared lest He come and we are not ready. This brings a soberness into life which leaves no room for idle talk and careless living. We learn to seek His will and to obey Him gladly. This in itself brings a present reward, because it produces in us a beauty and a grace which can only be achieved by a life of obedience. Our lives will be adorned with the fruit of the Spirit, which is 'love, joy, peace, longsuffering, gentleness, goodness, faith, meekness, temperance'(Gal. 5:22,23).

Loving His appearing

Because we are the children of God, the fear of His coming and of the judgment are removed. We are able to look forward to these great events with calmness and a joy in our hearts. Thus we fill our lives with delight in doing the will of the Lord, just as if we were cleaning and preparing our home in expectation of a long awaited guest and dearly loved friend. There is a joy and a happiness in this preparation, as there ought also to be in our hearts as we look for His coming. We need not fear judgment, for we have an Advocate who stands for us at the right hand of God the Father Almighty.

It is wonderful to know as we live here on earth that we shall 'enter into this glorious estate'. When we look around and see the increasing effect of sin and the mounting hatred against the Church of Jesus Christ, it is good to remind ourselves that nothing can hinder the gathering together of God's people, and that He will come. What a day it will be when an astounded world, living for its own selfish ends, pouring its venom upon the children of God, will suddenly be confronted by Him and by His judgment. Rather than face the anger of God, men will cry in horror for the mountains to cover them. But it will be of no avail. The day of pride and arrogance will be over, and all glory and honour will be ascribed to Him. For the believer, his faith will be rewarded, and the victory will be secured for ever. Meanwhile, as we quietly continue on our pilgrimage, we know that there is a limit to man's disobedience, that there is a day appointed when God will bring all things to a close, and bring in the New Jerusalem: 'we should live... looking for that blessed hope, and the glorious appearing of the great God and our Saviour Jesus Christ' (Titus 2:12,13).

11

THE INHERITANCE

Now that we are here alive on this earth it is difficult for any of us to imagine that there was a time when we were not. We are so full of our thoughts, opinions, hopes and ideas, that it seems strange that there should ever have been a time when we were nothing. The physical pain we feel when hurt, the wounds we experience when offended, the relief when we are healed and the happiness when pleased, all make us very much aware that life is not a dream but a real existence. And now that we are here and are made increasingly aware of that fact, the problem of our continued existence becomes very real to us.

Sooner or later it dawns upon us that we do not live here for ever. The stark reality confronts us that relatives, friends and neighbours die. It does not take much thought on our part to conclude that one day we too shall die. What is the end of man then, with life and knowledge of existence born in his heart? Was he meant for this life alone, with no explanation, no fulfilment, no future? Job, when groping for an explanation of why he was suffering grievous family and material losses, pondered on the destiny of his soul. Comparing a man with a tree, he said: 'For there is hope of a tree, if it be cut down, that it will sprout again, and that the tender branch thereof will not cease. Though the root thereof wax old in the earth, and the stock thereof die in the ground; Yet through the scent of water it will bud, and bring forth boughs like a plant. But man dieth, and wasteth away: yea, man giveth up the ghost, and where is he?' (Job 14:7-10). Job could not envisage that the end of man could be less than that of a tree, which even after its end sprouts new life again. Hope begins to spring anew in his heart, as he comes to see that God has some better plan for man than a dismal grave. 'If a man die, shall he live again?' (Job 14:14).

An immortal soul

We are reminded very often in the Bible of the immortality of our souls. In the teaching of our Lord Jesus Christ especially, we are solemnly reminded and warned of the importance of considering our eternal destiny. In the Gospel of Luke a parable is related of a man who was completely preoccupied with his material welfare and comfort. He could think of nothing else. He was so successful that he did not have enough room for his produce. 'And he thought within himself, saying, What shall I do, because I have no room where to bestow my fruits? And he said, This will I do: I will pull down my barns, and build greater; and there will I bestow all my fruits and my goods. And I will say to my soul, Soul, thou hast much goods laid up for many years; take thine ease, eat, drink, and be merry' (Luke 12:17-19). The poverty of such a life appals us: did life really have no more meaning for him than that? To live for self-gratification stands out as being terribly unworthy and very unsatisfying. Scripture warns such a person that this is not the end of the matter: 'But God said unto him, Thou fool, this night thy soul shall be required of thee: then whose shall those things be, which thou hast provided?' (Luke 12:20). How easy it is for us to allow our lives to drift by, filling some barn with earthly riches, believing we are rich when actually we are poor. In summing up the parable of the rich fool, our Lord remarks, 'So is he that layeth up treasure for himself, and is not rich toward God' (Luke 12:21). How many of us are rich towards God, having learnt to draw on the riches of His grace?

Hell

The Bible teaches quite clearly the continued existence of the soul after death, in either hell or heaven. There is no annihilation of the unsaved soul, as some suggest. This is a sobering thought and worthy of our consideration. We are told that 'these shall go away into everlasting punishment' (Matt. 25:46). Their existence will be one of utter misery which knows no end, a condition of absolute hopelessness: 'the children of the kingdom shall be cast out into outer darkness: there shall be weeping and gnashing of teeth' (Matt. 8:12). There is no more reason for us to suppose that there is an end to the suffering of the unrighteous, than there is to suppose a termination to the joy of the righteous. There seems to be in many of the references a finality that allows for no reprieve. For example, in the story of the rich man and Lazarus. Lazarus the beggar, who suffered much during his life, enjoyed heaven after his death. A rich man, however, who in life had showed no mercy to Lazarus, finds himself in hell, and appeals to Abraham to let Lazarus bring him succour. To emphasise the finality of their respective states we have these words, 'between us and you there is a great gulf fixed: so that they which would pass from hence to you cannot; neither can they pass to us, that would come from thence' (Luke 16:26).

The state of the condemned sinner is one of great sorrow, for whereas on this earth he benefited indirectly from the care and providence of God to mankind, and the restraint of God's mercy on human behaviour, he has no such influence in hell. Although he never appreciated the beneficence of God whilst on earth, its absence in hell will be catastrophic to him. To be lost is a terrible thing. We dare not, we cannot neglect this gospel that brings us from darkness to light, from the course of this world and from Satan unto the Lord God.

And heaven

In the teaching of our Lord Jesus Christ and throughout the Scripture we are also taught of a place which is a place of blessedness and joy. It is the teaching about heaven, referred to in Scripture in so many beautiful ways. On one occasion the Saviour is addressing the disciples when Peter interrupts him. The Lord resuming his theme, reassures Peter at the same time, 'Let not your heart be troubled: ye believe in God, believe also in me. In my Father's house are many mansions: if it were not so, I would have told you. I go to prepare a place for you' (John 14:1,2). The apostle Peter, when writing to a church which knew something of the sufferings of persecution, encourages them to turn their gaze to what had been done for them, who they were, and where they were bound. In a passage of extreme beauty and tenderness he wrote: 'Blessed be the God and Father of our Lord Jesus Christ, which according to his abundant mercy hath begotten us again unto a lively hope by the resurrection of Jesus Christ from the dead, To an inheritance incorruptible, and undefiled, and that fadeth not away, reserved in heaven for you' (1 Peter 1:3,4). The uninterrupted happiness of the inhabitants of the heavenly Jerusalem is described in such a way that the believer is encouraged as he travels to his home with God through life and its afflictions. 'And God shall wipe away all tears from their eyes; and there shall be no more death, neither sorrow, nor crying, neither shall there be any more pain: for the former things are passed away' (Rev. 21:4).

A place

Heaven is a place and not merely a condition. The bodily ascension of the Lord Jesus Christ points to this, as He leaves one place for another. There are many references to believers being within the kingdom and the fold, and unbelievers being outside and in another place, which is a place of turmoil and misery. The references to 'my Father's house', and to 'the inheritance' in Peter's First Epistle amongst others, points to a definite place where we as believers shall live. We also have the wonderful promise that we shall have a new body at the appointed time of His glorious second coming – 'We shall be like Him' (1 John 3:2). We shall inherit heaven and the entire new creation: 'I saw a new heaven and a new earth: for the first heaven and the first earth were passed away; and there was no more sea... And I heard a great voice out of heaven saying, Behold, the tabernacle of God is with men, and he will dwell with them, and they shall be his people, and God himself shall be with them, and be their God' (Rev. 21:1,3).

Those who go there

We are told frequently in Scripture that it is the righteous, the believer, who will inherit eternal life: 'For God so loved the world, that he gave his only begotten Son, that whosoever believeth in him should not perish, but have everlasting life' (John 3:16). The happy estate of the Christian is that he will inherit this wonderful life and shall be with God eternally. Our fellowship and communion will be sweet indeed. It will be unhindered by earthly and human limitations. We shall be able to look on God and live, and enjoy Him for ever.

Eternal life is a gift from God to undeserving sinners, who have been forgiven and stand accepted in His sight because Jesus Christ has paid the penalty for their sin. 'For the wages of sin is death; but the gift of God is eternal life through Jesus Christ our Lord' (Rom. 6:23). We know that there is nothing that we can do to earn this life. It is ours solely by the grace of God. Salvation is by faith in Jesus Christ, not by our own efforts and good works. Yet we know that those who are saved by the grace of God have a path of obedience and good works to walk, and that this is ordained of God: 'we are his workmanship, created in Christ Jesus unto good works, which God hath before ordained that we should walk in them' (Eph. 2:10).

There are indications in Scripture that there will be degrees of bliss. In some way our obedience and good works will determine our reward, but at the same time it is important to remember that we shall be in heaven by grace alone, and that the good we perform is also by His grace alone. Nevertheless we shall be rewarded, even though we cannot deserve or merit the reward of ourselves: 'Now he that planteth and he that watereth are one: and every man shall receive his own reward according to his own labour' (1 Cor. 3:8). Yet the happiness and joy of each and every inhabitant will be full and complete.

The difference it makes

This knowledge of eternal life changes everything. It is as if everything is put into its right perspective. This life with its joys and sorrows, its encouragements and its disappointments, no longer dominates our hearts. Previously we believed the pursuit of immediate happiness to be all-important, and difficulties and tragedies were hindrances that beset us on the way. Envy would fill our hearts when we learnt of the material good fortune of others, and we would long that the same might be our lot. Our happiness inevitably had to depend, therefore, on what we had, or at least hoped to have before long. But now, when we are deprived of ordinary worldly gains, we are not crestfallen, because our prize is greater and higher; and can never be taken away from us. Even in times of material loss and of deepest despair, we are comforted that nothing is able to separate us from the love of God, and that no one can take our names from the Book of Life. In our lives there will appear a calmness in the face of all men and all circumstances. And the world, which lays so much store by the immediate and present joys, will be astounded.

Now we see that death is not the end. We know that whatever may come upon us now need not overwhelm us, for even though we may die, it is not the end. We can face death with this victorious cry: 'O death, where is thy sting? O grave, where is thy victory?... thanks be to God, which giveth us the victory through our Lord Jesus Christ' (1 Cor. 15:55,57). Because we believe this, our hearts will not despair. We know that all things are in the hand of God, and He is preparing us for our eternal home. Suffering, tribulations, poverty and pain take on a new meaning: they are not meaningless frustrations of our happiness, but they work together for our ultimate good. One day we shall be above the strife and with our God.

He by Himself hath sworn,
I on His oath depend:
I shall, on eagle's wings upborne,
To heaven ascend;
I shall behold His face,
I shall His power adore,
And sing the wonders of His grace
For evermore.

The effect of the assurance of heaven is profound upon our minds and our hearts. It brings a new dimension into our thinking, and its effect is deep upon our lives. We have a new and living hope that shines upon our path. This is no idle hope, like the possibilities and probabilities of the promises of men, but rather the certain hope that the promises of God are true and dependable, like Himself. We believe in the physical resurrection of Jesus Christ and the implications of this, that we too shall be like Him with our new bodies. 'For if we believe that Jesus died and rose again, even so them also which sleep in Jesus will God bring with him. For this we say unto you by the word of the Lord, that we which are alive and remain unto the coming of the Lord shall not prevent them which are asleep. For the Lord himself shall descend from heaven with a shout, with the voice of the archangel, and with the trump of God: and the dead in Christ shall rise first: Then we which are alive and remain shall be caught up together with them in the clouds, to meet the Lord in the air: and so shall we ever be with the Lord' (1 Thess. 4:14-17). Because we believe in the truth of His resurrection we are persuaded that we too shall live with Him. Life takes on a new meaning: we see ourselves as on a pilgrimage. We are in the world but not of the world. We do not pin our hopes to the fading things of the world, because now our hearts and affections are set elsewhere. Like Abraham the friend of God, we are sojourners, enjoying the fellowship of the Lord here and now, but journeying to our home. 'For he looked for a city which hath foundations, whose builder and maker is God' (Heb. 11:10).

The Christian Hope

Although there are times when it seems as if the unbeliever receives more than his share of joys, and the believer has to shoulder so much that is hard, yet as compared with the lasting joys of those who belong to the Lord the profit of the unbeliever is small. Moses came to a time in his life when he considered seriously the course that he would take. He chose the path of faith. 'By faith Moses, when he was come to years, refused to be called the son of Pharaoh's daughter; Choosing rather to suffer affliction with the people of God, than to enjoy the pleasures of sin for a season; Esteeming the reproach of Christ greater riches than the treasures in Egypt: for he had respect unto the recompense of the reward' (Heb. 11:24-26). It is because we see further than death and the grave that we have a more balanced view of events in our lives. What seems meaningless to the world, in our eyes has a purpose. Injustices lose their sting because we know that there is One who understands and is in control, and that one day we shall be with Him. What we fail to understand now will be revealed to us then, but meanwhile we trust Him and know that His promises are true.

The story of Job is an inspiration to us when we consider his sufferings, and how the light of life dawned upon him, bringing hope in the midst of despair: 'For I know that my redeemer liveth, and that he shall stand at the latter day upon the earth: and though after my skin worms destroy this body, yet in my flesh shall I see God' (Job 19: 25,26).

Whatever our abiding place on this earth may be, whether in humble cottage or stately palace; whatever our estate may be, poor and obscure or rich and influential, we know as believers that Jesus Christ lives, and that because He rose from the dead we shall be with Him, and our home will be in heaven. This no one is able to take away from us.

Vernon Higham

God's Workmanship

What happens to Christians?

Faith

The Conscience

The Mind

The Will

Forgiveness

Temptation

Love

Death

God's Workmanship

What happens to Christians?

Vernon Higham

It is common for Christians, when they understand the glory and majesty of the gospel, to be so excited and overflowing with joy that even their sternest critics notice the change in the way they live.

Vernon Higham is an experienced pastor. His book is designed to help Christians to maintain that change consistently in their lives, not by our own strength but through understanding and experiencing the resources that God puts at our disposal.

This book will engage your mind and feelings as you explore how God changes you throughout your spiritual journey onward though death.

'A warm, easy-to-read introduction to key Bible doctrines. I welcome the reprint of this God-centred book which has already, over the past 25 years, been a great help to many people.'

Rev. Dr. D. Eryl Davies, Principal, Evangelical Theological College of Wales

ISBN 1 85792 255 7

Give me that Joy

'Full of nuggets of spiritual gold.' **Derick Bingham**

John Tallach

Meditations for spiritual maturity

Give me that Joy

Meditations for Spiritual Maturity

John Tallach

The Church grew, in the first 9 chapters of Luke 'Acts of the Apostles', from a handful of disciples to thousands of believers. This devotional study draws valuable lessons from those historical events. We are promised in the Bible that God's purpose for us is to grow too, from the first shoots of faith to a wholesome, fruitful maturity and understanding.

John Tallach provides a thoroughly practical book that will be of great personal help to those who want to see spiritual growth in their lives.

Each short devotional section of this book contains 'think about it' and 'pray about it' sections so that you can take the lessons this book has to offer to your heart and change the way you life.

'...full of nuggets of spiritual gold...'

Derick Bingham

'...appeals to us to get out of our backwaters and be filled again, and go on being filled with the Holy Spirit.'

Jessie McFarlane

John Tallach is a Church of Scotland Minister in the Highlands and author of several books.

ISBN 1 85792 263 8

'I know you will enjoy her insights in this poignant and personal book.'
Joni Eareckson Tada

ELEONORE VAN HAAFTEN

A REFUGE FOR MY HEART

Trusting God Even When Things Go Wrong

Foreword by J. I. Packer

A Refuge For My Heart

Trusting God Even When Things Go Wrong

Eleonore van Haaften

Looking at the lives of Naomi, Ruth, Joseph, Leah and David, van Haaften show us how the situations they had to face – loss, childlessness, rejection, loneliness – are still common today, and shows us what God's protection really means. Taking refuge in him is shown to be essential to our spiritual well being.

'All our hearts need constant overhaul, and I cannot imagine the Christian who will not be enriched by what is written here.'

J.I. Packer

'This book... has indeed been A Refuge for My Heart, reminding me to hide in God. It has indeed been balm for my soul.'

Elisabeth Elliot

'This moving book will be of great help to all Christians.'

Elizabeth Catherwood

'I know you will enjoy her insights in this poignant and personal book.'

Joni Eareckson Tada

Eleonore van Haaften is a much-respected international speaker from the Netherlands.

ISBN 1 85792 6846

"Personal, warm, real and challenging. I recommend a daily splash in the face."
Jerry Jenkins

VICTORIOUS
CHRISTIAN LIVING

SAMMY TIPPIT

Victorious Christian Living

Sammy Tippit

Do you find yourself having to ask forgiveness for the same sins over and over again? Is it possible to see victory over our old habits and ways?

Sammy Tippit is clear in his answer – YES

With short, punchy chapters covering sins including anger, deceit and temptation we are shown that by surrendering ourselves to Christ completely, and relying on him alone, the Christian Life can be victorious.

'Being biblical and Christ-centred has become second nature to this gifted brother, but when you consider the vulnerability and honesty not often seen in the writings of many evangelical leaders, you'll find you get more than you bargained for here. I recommend a daily splash in the face.'

Jerry B. Jenkins

'Sammy Tippit not only draws us into God's Word, but also opens a window so that we can see into his own heart. You will be blessed as you learn how God works in our lives.'

Dr. Erwin W. Lutzer

Sammy Tippit is an internationally renowned evangelist who has preached to hundreds of thousands at a time in countries as diverse as Mongolia, Brazil and Rwanda.

ISBN 1 85792 645 5

Christian Focus Publications

publishes books for all ages

Our mission statement –

STAYING FAITHFUL

In dependence upon God we seek to help make His infallible word, the Bible, relevant. Our aim is to ensure that the Lord Jesus Christ is presented as the only hope to obtain forgiveness of sin, live a useful life and look forward to heaven with Him.

REACHING OUT

Christ's last command requires us to reach out to our world with His gospel. We seek to help fulfill that by publishing books that point people towards Jesus and help them to develop a Christ-like maturity. We aim to equip all levels of readers for life, work, ministry and mission.

Books in our adult range are published in three imprints.

Christian Focus contains popular works including biographies, commentaries, basic doctrine, and Christian living. Our children's books are also published in this imprint.

Mentor focuses on books written at a level suitable for Bible College and seminary students, pastors, and other serious readers. The imprint includes commentaries, doctrinal studies, examination of current issues, and church history.

Christian Heritage contains classic writings from the past.

For a free catalogue of all our titles, please write to

Christian Focus Publications, Ltd
Geanies House, Fearn,
Ross-shire, IV20 1TW, Scotland, United Kingdom
info@christianfocus.com

For details of our titles visit us on our website

www.christianfocus.com